Supporting the IEP Process: A Facilitator's Guide

"A clearly written and practical guide to IEP facilitation . . . loaded with examples drawn from experience with special education negotiations."

—**Art Stewart,**
Coordinator of Mediation, Virginia Department of Education;
Senior Advisor, CADRE, Trainer and Consultant

"This informative guide, complete with practical simulations of how an effective facilitator can enhance communication and solution-building, has the potential to transform the IEP process."

—**Kate Scorgie, Ph.D.,**
Professor, Azusa Pacific University

"For anyone whose goal is to have the IEP process result in the optimal education programs for students with disabilities, Nick's book is a must read. All the information needed to keep a group of parents and professionals focused, productive, and working as a team are included."

—**Peggy Blanton,**
former Director of Special Education,
Fayette County Public Schools, Kentucky

"The next best thing to having Nick Martin at your side is to purchase this guidebook. It fosters what people appreciate most often—being good listeners and guiding the way to help others get to appropriate decisions. Diplomacy and support of feelings at its best!"

—**Nori Cuellar Mora, Ed.D.,**
former Associate Director of Instructional Services,
Education Service Center, Region 2, Corpus Christi, Texas

"Martin's simple and practical strategies provide the basis for facilitators to support recognition, empowerment and dialogue among team members to achieve meaningful collaboration."

—**Kathy Wian, MPA,**
Coordinator, Conflict Resolution Program, University of Delaware

"Nicholas Martin has once again provided a valuable resource in support of effective collaboration in Special Education. If you are considering serving in the role of IEP Facilitator or implementing a Facilitation system, you MUST read this book."

—**Gregory Abell,**
Senior Partner, Sound Options Group, LLC

"A practical, step by step guide for IEP Facilitators, Martin's book is also an excellent resource for states interested in designing or refining an IEP Facilitation program."

—**Kerry Voss Smith, Esquire,**
Director, Pennsylvania Office for Dispute Resolution

"Martin is very knowledgeable and is excellent at training people to be facilitators . . . I highly recommend the book for those who want to become facilitators or learn about facilitation."

—**Chuck Noe, M.A.,**
Member, Texas Council Administrators of Special Education

"The need for a practical guide for facilitators such as this cannot be underestimated. . . . This guide is positive, with an aim at better understanding by, and communication among, all parties."

—**Barbara C. Trolley, Ph.D., CRC,**
Professor, Counselor Education, St. Bonaventure University

"A practical tool, easy to read, and a must have for both school staff and parents…models valuable strategies for conflict prevention and resolution."

—**Patty Moore,**
Children, Family & Advocacy Services,
Alpha Resource Center of Santa Barbara, CA

Supporting the
IEP Process

Supporting the
IEP Process

A Facilitator's Guide

by

Nicholas R.M. Martin, M.A.

The Center for Accord, Inc.
Roanoke, Texas

·P A U L·H·
BROOKES
PUBLISHING C⁰ ®

Baltimore • London • Sydney

Paul H. Brookes Publishing Co.
Post Office Box 10624
Baltimore, Maryland 21285-0624
USA

www.brookespublishing.com

Typeset by Broad Books, Baltimore, Maryland.
Manufactured in the United States of America by
Versa Press, Inc., East Peoria, Illinois.

The individuals described in this book are composites of real people whose situations are masked, and they are based on the author's experience. Whenever appropriate to protect confidentiality, names and identifying details have been changed.

Library of Congress Cataloging-in-Publication Data

Martin, Nicholas R. M., 1951–
    Supporting the IEP process : a facilitator's guide / by Nicholas R.M. Martin.
        p.   cm.
    Includes bibliographical references and index.
    ISBN-13: 978-1-59857-114-1 (pbk.)
    ISBN-10: 1-59857-114-1
    1. Individualized education programs.   2. Group facilitation.   3. Communication in education.   I. Title.

    LC4019.M32   2010
    371.9'043–dc22   2010005208

British Library Cataloguing in Publication data are available from the British Library.

2014   2013   2012   2011   2010

10   9   8   7   6   5   4   3   2   1

Contents

About the Author

Nicholas R.M. Martin, M.A., is a conflict resolution consultant who lives near Fort Worth, Texas. Nick is a graduate of the University of Pennsylvania and the University of Hartford, and his educational background is in clinical psychology. After many years as a juvenile court psychologist, mental health counselor, and dispute mediator, he has come to focus increasingly on team building and conflict prevention in special education. He has had the opportunity to provide professional training in a great many states, which has given him helpful perspectives into the nationwide similarities, and at times regional differences, as parents and school personnel work together to live the vision of federal law: decision-making partnership for the benefit of children with special needs.

Nick has been providing highly acclaimed and practically oriented training for more than 30 years. He has also taught dispute resolution at the graduate school level. He is the author of *An Operator's Manual for Successful Living,* now in its second edition (The Center for Accord, Inc., 2008). His other major works include *Strengthening Relationships When Our Children Have Special Needs* (Future Horizons, 2004, also available in Spanish) and *A Guide to Collaboration for IEP Teams* (Paul H. Brookes Publishing, 2005). He has also published numerous newspaper and journal articles, some of which can be found at his web site, www.4accord.com.

Preface

From a background in clinical psychology and mental health counseling, I have discovered that there is in our culture a chronic weakness in the all-important area of the emotional side of living. We simply don't understand enough about feelings—where they come from, how they manifest, what they represent, and, most important, how to handle them effectively. It is this, more than any other factor, that I believe underlies conflict in special education, just as it underlies conflict in any other area of human relationships. Somebody feels bad, whether it be hurt, scared, belittled, disrespected, or so forth. And then what do they do? Do they file a complaint or a lawsuit, walk away mad, become demanding or abusive, or perhaps seethe in silence? Because emotions are the driving force—the animator—of human behavior, they become a critical factor in the individualized education program (IEP) process. Whether IEP team meetings run smoothly or not will have everything to do with how the participants feel, how they express their feelings, and how everyone involved is able to be sensitive and responsive to the *feelings* of those seated around the table.

All of this was explored in some depth in my book, *A Guide to Collaboration for IEP Teams* (Martin, 2005). That book outlined the steps necessary for special education planning committees to work together effectively for the benefit of children, with a maximum of team spirit and a minimum of conflict. This book is, in some ways, a sequel to that one, and yet it differs in one very important regard: the IEP team participant for whom this information is intended. That is, my previous work was aimed primarily at the *chairperson* of the IEP committee, the one responsible for leading the team at the IEP meeting. However, many of those skills and practices are equally relevant for the *other* members of the team, as well. Although it is the chairperson who must, for example, ensure that preconferencing occurs, an agenda is in place, introductions are made, the time is well managed, and so forth, many elements of the IEP environment are just as much the responsibility of all of the participants. These include coming prepared; being on time; and being courteous, respectful, on task, and professional. It is also essential that *all* members, not just the chairperson, be diplomatic and tactful, understand how to communicate and collaborate, and know how to use their differences creatively in order to reach a consensus that serves the best interests of the child. Although more could be said, the point is simply to emphasize that my previous work, *A Guide to Collaboration for IEP Teams,* was intended to be just what its title suggests: a practical manual for working together effectively, efficiently, and with a minimum of conflict. This work is different. Although this book relies on the same principles of collaboration, consensus building, and conflict prevention, the intended audience is primarily the new kid on the IEP block: the facilitator—an impartial outsider who supports the team but is not a member of the team. And yet the same skill set that allows the facilitator to bring a great deal that is new and valuable will also be useful to the team members, as well. That is, *any member* can enhance the collaborative potential of the IEP team by using the skills that will be presented here.

Although not a requirement under law, many states have found that conflict in special education can be greatly reduced by providing the assistance of a trained and impartial facilitator. This added participant at IEP meetings offers many advantages. The most obvious, as documented in Chapter 6, is a very high level of agreement on IEPs. And if one considers that facilitation is usually requested for potentially *contentious* meetings, its high success rate is particularly significant. Other benefits include reduced conflict, increased trust and team spirit, more positive relationships, and the avoidance of escalation into costly legal activity. Perhaps the greatest benefit, albeit one not so easily measured, is the support that facilitation of IEP meetings offers to the vision of special education law—that these committees will act in decision-making *partnership.* ("Changes in the law [Individuals with Disabilities Education Act Amendments of 1997, PL 105-17] represent an effort to ensure that school officials consider parents as decision-making partners in the undertaking of providing special education and related services to their child," Abt Associates, 2002, p. 32.)

Some readers may be interested to know the background of this project—how this book came about and what qualifies me to write on this subject. These are fair questions and not difficult to answer.

My background is in clinical psychology, in which I completed a master's degree in 1975 at the University of Hartford after receiving a bachelor's degree from the University of Pennsylvania in 1973. As a very young 20-something, I was fortunate to have the opportunity to live my dream of being a psychologist and mental health counselor, first in juvenile corrections and then in outpatient mental health. After a few years, however, I found myself becoming disenchanted with my chosen career track and with psychotherapy in general. The word *psychotherapy* comes from the Greek and means "healing of the mind" or "therapy of the psyche." Yet in my work in juvenile corrections, I was finding that most of the children "sent upstate" were not bad kids or sick kids—they were troubled kids, very often lacking in basic social skills, most notably communication. From this lack of ability to express themselves well then emerged a host of secondary problems—in terms of temper control, self-respect and respect for others, insecurity, depression, despair, and so on. Without the ability to meaningfully and positively effect change in their worlds through effective communication, they relied instead on other, less acceptable means of expressing their feelings and achieving their goals, not always with positive results. The "difficult" children were often sent to me, the staff psychologist, to intervene. I remember putting several of them in an assertiveness training group, and we role-played challenging situations from their everyday lives. Given more effective communication skills, they soon became model students! My "psychotherapy" had involved nothing more than *teaching* them how to communicate, and with that came a host of other benefits.

Later, as a community mental health counselor, I found that my practice came to increasingly revolve around three very simple questions. No matter who came in the door or what their presenting complaints, I found myself asking them, in effect, "When that happened, how did you feel? When you felt that way, what did you do? And when you did that, how did it work?" Invariably, their solutions weren't working very well (why else would they be coming to see me?), and so the next question became what they might do instead—how they might approach their challenges differently so as to get more favorable results. Nine times out of ten, their best option involved developing skills in effective communication. In short, and once again, whatever the setting and whatever the problem, my psychotherapy was ultimately only education—private tutoring, in a sense, in awareness of feelings and of more productive options for their behavioral expression. And more than any other behavioral option, what my clients all seemed to be needing, just as the children in juvenile corrections, was more effective communication skills.

Is this a great departure from the subject of facilitation in special education? Well, people in conflict invariably feel bad. That is, they have unpleasant, or "negative," feelings, and one of the primary roles of the facilitator is to help them to express and resolve these feelings productively by helping them to *communicate* more effectively.

Once I woke up to the realization that my counseling work involved, more than anything, *educating* people in how to think and act differently so as to achieve more desirable results, I also came to realize that one-to-one counseling, or even small-group counseling, was an extremely costly and inefficient way to work! A different forum with larger numbers at lower cost seemed a better alternative. And so I began to be the staff person at the counseling center who responded to requests from the community for a speaker on any of a number of popular topics, such as stress management, self-esteem, effective communication skills, coping with burnout, a new life after divorce, and similar topics of interest. One of the most frequently requested topics was conflict resolution, and it was a few years later, at a training in conflict resolution skills, that a hand went up and an elementary school principal asked if I could train her IEP committee chairs.

At that time, I honestly had no idea what any of this was all about, and I consider her question to be my launch point into special education. I soon came to find that there is a federal requirement that a committee be formed whenever a child may have a need for specially designed instruction. I also learned that these committees are often hotbeds of conflict, usually between parents and school personnel. I learned that they are intended to work collaboratively toward consensus with a minimum of conflict but that very few of the participants nationwide have received sufficient practical training in how to live this vision successfully. And so I developed a 2-day workshop titled "Collaboration in the IEP Environment," which has by now been presented to thousands of IEP participants in many states and has led in turn to the development of various other training programs related to special education and its associated challenges. As a result of the training I had been doing in special education, I received one day a most welcome and unexpected request: to develop a model curriculum for the training of IEP team facilitators in Texas! Facilitation was something other states had been doing with great success for some time, and it was now time to bring it to the Lone Star State.

I felt deeply honored to be given such an opportunity. I developed the training in 2007 and based it heavily on my experience as a trainer in (and observer of) the IEP team process. I also researched what was being done in other states and drew heavily from my mediation practice, which involved 12 years as a part-time court-connected mediator and a postal service mediator. I also had the chance to work and learn alongside the many school professionals who have been my students and to personally facilitate or observe the facilitation of IEP teams in the "real world." All of this has given me tremendous confidence in the facilitation process and also a clarity with regard to the specific skills necessary to make such facilitation work—and to work supremely well. I thank you, my reader, for giving me the opportunity to share this now with you.

REFERENCES

Abt Associates. (2002, July). *Study of state and local implementation and impact of the Individuals with Disabilities Education Act*. Retrieved January 14, 2010, from www.abt.sliidea.org/Reports/FSI_FinalRpt.doc

Individuals with Disabilities Education Act Amendments of 1997, PL 105-17, 20 U.S.C. §§ 1400 *et seq.*

Martin, N.R.M. (2005). *A guide to collaboration for IEP teams*. Baltimore: Paul H. Brookes Publishing Co.

Introduction

In recent years, there has been an accelerating awareness of the need to move conflict "upstream" by providing alternatives for dispute resolution apart from the traditional methods that have been in place since the Education for All Handicapped Children Act (PL 94-142) was signed into law in 1975. This law has since evolved into the Individuals with Disabilities Education Improvement Act of 2004 (PL 108-446), and its purpose remains to safeguard the entitlement of all U.S. children to a free and appropriate public education in the least restrictive environment. Someone who believes that a child's rights under this law have been neglected or violated has long had two available means of addressing this. The first has been through a due process hearing—an administrative lawsuit to determine whether that which is due and proper under the law is, in fact, being done. The second has been through a formal complaint investigation, which allows anyone with doubts to request that the state department of education consider the concerns and, after careful review, issue a written response in a timely manner.

Due process hearings are extremely expensive; a single hearing is estimated to involve $50,000 in legal defense for school districts and perhaps $30,000 for parents who choose to hire attorneys to represent them. Both due process hearings and complaint investigations are also extremely time consuming, especially for school districts, and both are very much adversarial, often causing substantial harm to the all-important school–parent relationship on which the child depends for his or her education. Furthermore, both take the participants (school personnel and parents) out of the driver's seat, leaving decision making to the hearing officer or department of education staff who will determine the truth and establish a remedy.

Every few years the federal government reexamines its special education laws and issues a "reauthorization." In 1997, in recognition of these shortcomings, a major change with regard to conflict resolution was the addition of a requirement that all states must now provide mediation as an additional option for resolving special education disputes. In mediation, an impartial third person meets with the parties (usually the parents and school district representatives, often accompanied by attorneys) and gives them the opportunity to express their concerns and to work out an agreement that both sides can accept. Mediation is much quicker than due process hearings and complaint investigations and is far less adversarial and damaging to relationships. It also allows the parties themselves to remain the decision makers. If they do not like what they hear by way of settlement options, they do not have to accept them, and they can continue their dispute by means of a complaint investigation or due process hearing if they wish.

As is discussed in Chapter 6, mediation has been found to be extremely effective, with an estimated 75% success rate and an even higher satisfaction rate among those who take advantage of this option. And yet, despite all its benefits and advantages, most states seem to find that mediation is very much underutilized and that, in general, participants seem to be more willing to choose other alternatives (i.e., due process hearings or complaint investigations) before reaching for the *only* one that allows them to decide their own outcome.

Now, more than 12 years since the advent of mediation as an option under federal law, it has become obvious that mediation is not by itself proving sufficient to prevent the escalation of conflict in special education. Something more is obviously necessary. What might that be? Enter facilitation.

Facilitation is a process that enlists the support of a neutral party who can assist the IEP team to work more effectively and achieve its aims. As his or her role will be defined in this book, this third party is not an authority, not a decision maker, and not an expert, except perhaps in collaborative methods and how to go about using strong feelings and differences of opinion to actually *assist* teams to reach consensus. And the facilitator does not act as a mediator, although the skill sets required for these roles have a high degree of overlap.

All mediation can actually be considered a subset of facilitation to the extent that it is inherently a form of assisted dialogue. However, much like the proverbial "all rabbits are mammals but not all mammals are rabbits," not all facilitation is mediation, and in the context of special education, it is actually very different. First of all, facilitation takes place during a regularly scheduled meeting of the IEP team; it is not a separate meeting or a separate process. Second, it is not necessarily a dispute resolution option, as is mediation. That is, facilitation could be requested whenever team members think it might be helpful to have someone assist them to do their best work; there may be no dispute at all. Third, whereas mediation involves select representatives of the school district and of the child, facilitation works with the IEP team as a whole.

Simply stated, facilitation is a new option being made available in more and more states as they come to see from the experience of others that it provides a powerful and highly beneficial alternative to existing conflict resolution options. This is the subject of this book: the nature of facilitation, what facilitators do, and *how* facilitation can and will help IEP teams to succeed.

1 Fa-*cil*-i-tate:
vt. to make easier

Mother: I'm sorry, but *no.* I can't let you put my child in the general classroom when his doctor said that he should have one-to-one therapy.

Speech therapist: Mrs. Garcia, there is a lot of evidence that shows that children learn a great deal from their peers—things they don't pick up when they are in a more contrived environment. Only giving him one-to-one services in self-contained is just not going to give him the same benefits he would get if he were interacting with other kids in a real-world scenario doing their normal activities and speaking not so much to him as just around him. I don't think it would hurt him in any way. It would be additional, not instead of, for maybe a few sessions each week.

Mother: Well, I'm just not going to agree to that. He should have one-to-one.

Diagnostician: Mrs. Garcia, I think what Mrs. Franklin is trying to say is that there are a lot of children on the spectrum with audio-linguistic delay, and we have seen lots of progress from a general classroom setting that we just don't see when a child's only modeling comes from an adult in a therapeutic setting or in a behavior unit.

Mother: *(shakes head)* No. That's not what I want for him. I don't want to put him in the classroom. I want him to continue working with Mrs. Johnson. He likes her and they get along fine, and I don't want to be changing things on him now.

Assistant principal: *(as an eerie silence befalls the group)* I understand what you're saying, but you need to understand the responsibility we have to provide the services that are going to best meet his needs. If you would just be a little more flexible, ma'am, I think you would see that this is something that will only help your son. We need to be thinking a little more positively here. *(smiles reassuringly)*

Mother: *(with some irritation)* I already told you, I'm not going to agree to the classroom. If you want to do that when I said I don't want it, then we will just have to see what happens next, because it's not going to be that way. I already told you.

Assistant principal: Mrs. Garcia, we are only trying to help your child. We have cleared our schedules and arranged to be here for this meeting. People have put a lot of time into preparing for this meeting, and our only desire is to help your son. And now you are *threatening* us? The problem here is that you don't understand the situation and you won't let us do what needs to be done. This is not for *our* benefit. This is for your son. So I guess if you want to see your child continue to lag further and further behind, well, I'm sorry, Mrs. Garcia, there's just not a lot more we can do.

(Mother picks up her purse and leaves without response.)

Special education teacher: Gosh, that lady can be so rigid.

Speech therapist: I don't think she heard a single thing we were trying to say.

Assistant principal: The problem with these parents is they just don't understand the situation. They have no formal training, but they can come in here making whatever demands they want to, and we're supposed to just fall in step.

Special education teacher: It's the kids that are suffering for this. That's who I feel bad for.

Classroom teacher: I'm sorry, team, but I have to get back to my classroom. I suppose now we have to schedule *another* meeting?

As an exercise, participants in facilitation training are asked to jot down a few notes about individualized education program (IEP) scenarios that they have found to be particularly difficult, unpleasant, or unproductive. Many of them will think back to IEP meetings that may have been very similar to the scenario here. They are then asked to consider three questions: What happened? What was the source of the problem? What might have helped?

The opening scenario here is not meant to be a model of best practices by any means. However, it does illustrate a number of features that all too often characterize contentious IEP meetings. It also offers a starting point for examining the unique role that a neutral facilitator who is not a decision-making member of the team can play in assisting members to move through their obstacles and achieve consensus in most cases (75% or more; see Chapter 6).

In the sample scenario, the mother was unwilling to accept the advice of all her other teammates, and they in turn were frustrated that she did not seem to be listening and that she then left when she did not get her way. This might be the response to that question of "What happened?"—in other words, what were the facts, and who said what?

But what was really the *source* of the problem? No doubt people will recall a difficult, unpleasant, or unproductive IEP meeting primarily because of what happened—the behaviors. And yet where did those behaviors come from? What is it that led the participants to choose to say or do whatever it is they did?

In the sample scenario, perhaps it was a history of bad feelings and mistrust on the part of the mother and a history of frustration on the part of school personnel. Perhaps it was a lack of real understanding of why each of the speakers had adopted the position he or she had taken with regard to what was best for the child. Was it perhaps the absent doctor, who was steering the mother without being present to participate, explain, or reconsider? Was it maybe a feeling of intimidation and powerlessness on the mother's part and a belief that only the intervention of a higher authority could lead to a successful outcome? Or was it perhaps a lack of training and skill? Clearly, the team members demonstrated a limited understanding of how to work through their seemingly impossible differences—they didn't seem to know their options when they found themselves disagreeing about the things that were important to them. In all probability, the real source of the problem was all of the above.

The next question, then, is what might have helped? Would more effective communication—or greater sensitivity, compassion, or tactfulness—have made any difference? Would open minds have been helpful? Or trusting that the group's collaborative process would see them through this hard place? Would it have helped if team members had better understood one another's points of view and known how to go about bringing those perspectives to light? Did the members have options when it came to expressing their frustrations or changing one another's minds? Was their failure to reach agreement really inevitable? Would *every* team with similar challenges have ended up the exact same way?

The responses of IEP team members to these three questions (What happened? What was the source of the problem? and What would have helped?) are many and varied. Yet typical responses of school personnel to the second question include

- Preset agendas, such that people come locked into certain positions (Didn't the mother in the preceding scenario come locked into the position of only one-to-one services? Weren't the school personnel locked into believing the general classroom was best?)

- Hidden agendas, such that the real issues and concerns are not made clear (Do the other team members really know what is motivating the mother's inflexibility?)

- Differing views on what is necessary (one-to-one services versus modeling in the classroom setting; clearly evident in this scenario)
- Outsiders who steer participants into certain positions or later undermine their agreements (The doctor has obviously influenced the mother, and yet he is not present to participate in the discussions.)
- Past dissatisfactions and disappointments (When the special education teacher says "that lady can be so rigid," it seems likely that there has been a history of difficulties and frustrations.)
- Belligerent attitudes and closed minds (Both are evident in the scenario.)
- Staff who are caught unawares, not prepared for what is being said or asked (also evident)
- Unreasonable or inappropriate expectations (also evident)
- Fear, anger, and mistrust (also evident)

Of course, a single scenario is not going to capture every one of the underlying sources of challenge in the IEP environment, but quite a few of these challenges are reflected in the preceding example. Like "threads that run so true," many of these obstacles are very common, even though the specifics can be as different as the participants involved.

Given such a long list of challenges, is there nothing that could have been done? When asked "What might have helped?" school personnel often propose the following suggestions. Many fit well with the sample scenario here, especially the intervention points at the end.

Positive Attitudes and Mutual Understanding

- Remembering the child and the team members' common goals and objectives
- Helping the team members to see one another's perspectives more clearly
- Shifting from having negative expectations to believing in possibilities
- Understanding the child, the law, and the resources available

Preconferencing

- Knowing beforehand what concerns will be shared and what demands will be made
- Limiting the number of participants, yet ensuring that those required *are* present and prepared
- Having good documentation and the necessary data for the decisions to be made
- Having clarity with regard to roles and responsibilities

Meeting Structure

- Practicing effective time management
- Establishing ground rules
- Clarifying goals and objectives
- Arriving on time
- Staying for the entire meeting
- Using a written agenda
- Staying focused
- Explaining the process
- Having summaries and overviews available

Communication

- Remaining professional and respectful
- Speaking in plain language
- Welcoming each member to share
- Listening well and helping each member feel heard
- Acknowledging feelings
- Maintaining a problem-solving focus
- Encouraging positive discussion
- Avoiding blame and attack

Intervention Points

- Having priorities right
- Revealing hidden agendas
- Countering preconceptions
- Enforcing ground rules
- Managing anger and other emotions
- Drawing out the expertise of the group
- Understanding resources and options
- Redirecting grudges and "baggage" toward resolution
- Avoiding demonizing
- Emphasizing the positive
- Maintaining open minds and flexibility
- Promoting mutual understanding
- Exploring interests
- Being willing to consider different options
- Giving something a trial period to see if it will help
- Not letting the team give up too easily

- Handling impasse
- Working effectively with advocates
- Rebuilding damaged relationships
- Restoring trust

With this as a general overview of the perspectives shared by school professionals, one can begin to see the areas where IEP team members get into difficulty and what would, at such a time, be helpful. Chapters 5 and 6 refer back to the sample scenario about speech services and bring into focus some critical junctures for intervention. Chapters 5 and 6 also explore some of the many options available to the group that would probably have led to a more successful outcome.

REACHING AGREEMENT

When people are working together toward agreement, they may use any of a variety of methods, not all of which have much to recommend them. When asked how people *typically* make agreements, school professionals will often say such things as by consensus, according to what's best for the child, or according to laws and policies. And yet when groups are observed making decisions, they do not always follow these praiseworthy methods. Instead, some of the following processes are often used, although not always consciously and intentionally.

The Big Dog Method

The first method of decision making, and perhaps one of the most common, could be called "the big dog method." Here, the vocal minority leads the group. That is, those who think most quickly and speak most openly steer the group, while those who are more reflective and less outspoken may just follow along. Among the many downsides of this method is that the vocal minority may not always represent the views of the majority or the greater wisdom of the group as a whole, and those who silently disagree may feel dissatisfied or resentful and may not really support the decisions that have been made.

Intimidation

Another common method, although obviously not recommended, is winning through intimidation. Threats and belligerence may lead others to give in and go along, even when the proposal is not the best and the team is not at all in agreement.

Compromise

In a compromise, everyone gets part of what they want but no one gets all of what they want. Team members have met in the middle, which may seem very fair and may even be acceptable to them. Yet it may not be ideal, and all members may walk away feeling less than satisfied with the outcome. A simple story that illustrates the shortcomings of compromise is that of the lone orange remaining in the bowl.

> ### The Lone Orange
>
> Two children are quarrelling over the lone orange remaining in the bowl. From another room, Dad overhears them bickering: "I want it!—But I got here first—But you always get what you want—But I need it more than you do—But you got the last one!" Dad gets up, walks into the kitchen, and asks the girls to give him the orange. He then reaches for a sharp knife, cuts the orange in half, and offers them each an equal part of the orange. To his surprise, however, the girls burst into tears, explaining that one wanted the peel of a whole orange to follow her cake recipe, whereas the other wanted the fruit of a whole orange to follow a different cake recipe. By cutting the orange in half, Dad ensured that neither girl had what she needed to achieve her objectives.

In this story, both of the daughters could have had *all* that they wanted if Dad had first understood not just what they wanted but also *why* (in other words, if he had taken the time to understand their *interests*). This is the foundation of *principled negotiation,* a highly effective yet simple model for building consensus and one that is explored in greater detail in Chapters 3 and 5. It serves as a wonderful illustration of how compromise is not just one of many options but how it can sometimes be the *worst* option!

Majority Rule

Another common route to agreement is by vote, with the majority winning and thereby "ruling." Like compromise, this method is held in very high regard in Western culture, and yet, despite all its advantages, it usually results in winners and losers and the bad feelings that typically go along with losing. It may also leave the thoughts and concerns of the losing minority unaddressed while failing to incorporate their wisdom into the decision of the group as a whole.

Third-Party Decision (Arbitration)

Examples of third-party decision makers include judges in court, chain of command and higher level administrators, and parents who settle disputes for their children. Again, with third-party decision makers there will always be winners and losers, as well as the hard feelings that tend to go along with being on the losing side. Also, the potential will be lost for all views to be heard and incorporated into a mutually determined, mutually agreed-upon, and mutually acceptable solution.

What these five methods of reaching agreement have in common is that they all reflect what has been called "position-based bargaining." The focus is on the thing that those in disagreement want, and the decision-making method determines which of the opposing sides gets whatever is in dispute. The story of the lone orange reflects this: The focus was the orange, and the decision-making process revolved around who would get all or part of it. When the girls' big dog and intimidation methods failed, Dad, a third-party decision maker, stepped forward to impose compromise in an effort to settle the dispute. All of these are in marked contrast to *collaboration toward consensus,* in which the parties themselves are the decision makers and nobody wins until everybody wins—that is, no decision is made until everyone is willing to agree. Such collaboration has many undeniable benefits.

BENEFITS OF CONSENSUS-BASED DECISION MAKING

One benefit of consensus-based decision making is that it addresses the *spirit* of the law: It is the clear intention of federal law that IEP team participants work *as partners* (e.g., ". . . parents of children with disabilities are encouraged by the [Individuals with Disabilities Education Act Amendments of 1997, PL 105-17] to work in other ways as partners with educators and policymakers"; Abt Associates, 2002, p. 32). Moreover, it is only through consensus that all participants will have ownership of the decisions they have made; therefore, team members will be more likely to support them and see them through to completion. Positive feelings, mutual trust, and positive team spirit are all by-products of true collaboration and consensus, something that is far less assured and often impossible by any other method. In addition, the wisdom of the group is pooled and all viewpoints are heard and incorporated into the final outcome. Furthermore, and very important, consensus-based decision making has none of the "harmful side effects" of the methods described previously: losers, bad feelings, lack of support and endorsement, or neglecting of important perspectives.

There is only one known shortcoming of consensus-based decision making, and that is that it requires *time.* It is not always the easiest method, and it is certainly not the quickest; yet in many settings it can and does work extremely well. Whenever a relatively small group of people share a common purpose and can collectively bring the necessary knowledge and understanding to the table, collaboration toward consensus is ideal. The IEP environment is just such a setting in which it really can shine—for the benefit of all of the team members and the child for whom they are meeting.

WHAT HELPS ACHIEVE CONSENSUS?

Having established that consensus is the best of all avenues for decision making at IEP meetings, the next logical question, then, is what will help teams to achieve it? Here are seven key elements that promote collaboration toward consensus.

> ### Keys to Collaboration
>
> 1. Remembering the common purpose
> 2. Giving everyone a voice
> 3. Communicating openly yet with respect
> 4. Assuming good reason and intention
> 5. Exploring underlying interests
> 6. Valuing the team and its members
> 7. Trusting the process

Let's return to the long list of challenges reported by IEP team participants (summarized on p. 4). Most, if not all, reflect something missing from this simple list of elements that make for success. Not surprisingly, most of the recommendations for what might have helped in those situations fall neatly under these same seven categories. *This* is what must be brought to the table to help the IEP team process run more smoothly. This is the answer to the question "What would have helped?" And this is the work of the facilitator—to help IEP teams succeed by creating or restoring these seven elements that promote collaboration. *How* the facilitator can do this is the subject of this book.

2 | Three Philosophies of Helping
Facilitator Styles

In beginning a discussion of how a facilitator can help an individualized education program (IEP) committee to succeed, it may be helpful to review three philosophies of helping that have become somewhat standardized. That is, three styles have come to be recognized with regard to the approach of "the neutral"—the unbiased third party who assists the two or more sides in a decision-making process to reach an agreement. Although these styles are associated primarily with mediation, there is great overlap in the skill sets that make for successful mediators and facilitators. In fact, all mediation *is* facilitation in that all mediation is essentially facilitated dialogue. All mediation and all facilitation involve the assistance of an impartial third party who helps the others by supporting their discussion. The main difference is that mediation usually involves two clearly defined parties and a clearly defined dispute—for example, mediation between a petitioner and a respondent in a lawsuit. In contrast, facilitation may involve any number of parties, those parties may or may not be clearly defined, and there may be no dispute at all. For example, a facilitator may be asked to assist a neighborhood association with deciding whether to permit drilling for natural gas on its green space; there could be tens or hundreds of participants, and one or many issues, but no defined sides and perhaps no dispute at all—only discussion.

Before presenting the standard approaches facilitators use, it may be worth clarifying the meaning of the term *facilitator*. This word is used in many contexts and can easily conjure a variety of images. School professionals often use the term (or the similar term *internal facilitator*) to refer to the chairperson, leader, coordinator, or manager of the IEP team. It is this person's responsibility to guide the meeting, lead the team in the development of the IEP, ensure that appropriate records are kept, and ensure that all legal requirements are met.

However, in this book, that person is referred to as the *chairperson*. Although the chairperson does assist and support communication during the meeting, his or her role is very different from that of the facilitator, even though he or she may use many of the same skills. The key difference, at least as the term will be used throughout this book, is that the facilitator is not a decision maker and is not a member of the IEP team; instead, he or she is a neutral party, attending solely for the purpose of assisting the team members to collaborate effectively.

Others use the term *facilitator* to refer to an outside expert, perhaps a district specialist or a special education administrator, who joins an IEP meeting to assist with the decision-making process and perhaps assist with communication and conflict resolution. Although this person may, again, use many of the same skills, his or her role differs from the facilitator's role described in this book if he or she has authority over any members of the committee and/or will not be truly impartial.

The use of facilitation at IEP meetings is a "new kid on the block," and its definition is sure to evolve as its use becomes more widespread and more standardized, and as greater understanding is gained. In fact, a precise definition of the role and limitations of the facilitator is a topic that is much debated in professional circles.

With that said, a discussion of facilitation can perhaps best begin by exploring three commonly accepted philosophies of the impartial helper, which include evaluative, facilitative, and transformative. In comparing and contrasting these three approaches, it is important to keep in mind that the summaries presented here are not necessarily *recommended* methods. Rather, in the context of facilitation in the IEP environment, they may serve as a backdrop from which to begin to formulate a philosophy that can truly be considered "best practice."

EVALUATIVE FACILITATION

In the evaluative model, the facilitator is an outside expert who brings to the table knowledge and skills that help move the group toward agreement. The evaluative facilitator may give information, advise the team members, and predict what is likely to happen if settlement is not reached. In the special education arena, such an evaluative facilitator is able to forecast, based on experience, what would probably happen at a due process hearing or a formal complaint investigation. The evaluative facilitator is powerful, and he or she leads the meeting and directs the group members along the pathways by which they are most likely to reach an agreement, hence the alternative name for this approach: directive.

In the legal arena, the evaluative approach is most common among attorney mediators and retired judges, who are usually selected precisely because of their knowledge of the law, experience at trial, and ability to help the parties understand the strengths and weaknesses of their case *before* they run the risk of losing before a judge or jury in court.

The evaluative facilitator may propose options for the team to consider and might even recommend a particular course of action. After all, that is what he or she has been asked or hired to do—to provide additional expertise that will help the team reach agreement. As one evaluative mediator phrased it, "I don't represent either side. I'm here to represent the settlement." Not surprisingly, this approach is also called *settlement driven* because its goal is to enable the parties to enter into agreements that will settle their dispute. Note, however, that the facilitator or mediator in this model is not a decision maker. Only the group decides whether settlement occurs and, if so, in what form. Yet the mark of success is whether settlement is reached. When a school district sends an administrator or expert to help the IEP team, that person will often (and rightly) use an evaluative approach—helping the team to consider, explore, and evaluate which of several different ideas and options will serve the student best while also helping the team better understand its legal obligations.

FACILITATIVE FACILITATION

Although this may seem like confusing double-talk, it is really very meaningful to talk about the "facilitative" approach to intervention. One can think of it as the process of facilitation according to the *facilitative* model.

In the facilitative approach, the facilitator supports the process of the team. He or she may guide the group but not direct it; may ask questions but not advise; may share information but not imply what the group *should* do. Even if the facilitator has an opinion or knows what might happen if the matter were taken to a higher level, it would be out of bounds for him or her to say so. If pressed ("C'mon, you know more than you're telling us!"), the facilitative facilitator would probably respond with something along the lines of "Well, I'm not here as an expert today; I'm only here to support your process. What do *you* think? Or might there be someone you could call to get that information?"

This doesn't mean the facilitator is passive, silent, or evasive. The facilitator can be very vocal and very active. He or she might ask probing questions to encourage the group to consider different options and their implications (e.g., "What would you think about an independent evaluation?" or "Have you thought of trying a behavioral intervention plan in the classroom?"). Thus, the facilitator might participate in option generation by adding possibilities that the group members may not have thought of themselves. In a sense, the facilitator is a member of the team for the day. (In this context, *member* means *participant*—not a decision-making or legal member of the IEP committee and not a signatory to the IEP.) Yet, unlike an evaluative/directive facilitator, the facilitative neutral does not give opinions and is very careful not to imply a right or wrong answer; that is only for the team to decide. Furthermore, the goal of the facilitative model is not settlement. Rather, it is productive dialogue. The facilitative facilitator supports the group in communicating effectively and exploring its various options, but it is entirely up to the group members themselves whether they wish to settle the matter.

Before moving on to the third approach, it is important to emphasize that within the facilitative model is a spectrum of possible interventions and a wide range of options. Some of these options support only the decision-making *process* of the team, whereas others permit much more active involvement in the "content" of the discussions. This process–content distinction will become more clear in a moment and is discussed in detail in Chapters 5 and 7.

TRANSFORMATIVE FACILITATION

The transformative model is based on the teachings of Bush and Folger (1994), authors of the well-known book *The Promise of Mediation.* The book's subtitle neatly summarizes the purpose of the transformative method: "responding to conflict through empowerment and recognition."

The transformative model could also be called *reflective.* The transformative facilitator does not lead or direct the group at all. Instead, he or she simply reflects to the group what the members are saying or doing. In this model, the facilitator follows the group, making statements more than asking questions, such as "This issue seems to be very important to you," or "I sense some frustrations among the team members." When the facilitator does ask questions, the purpose is not to encourage the group to think of possibilities they may not yet have thought of but rather to ask for decision and direction (e.g., "So where would you like to go with that?" or "What would you like to do now?"). The facilitator is never the one to provide direction but instead encourages the group members to establish their own. Thus, the facilitator does not propose options even if he or she might know of some. The facilitator sees himself or herself as powerless; it is the group that is powerful. The facilitator's role is to serve as a "magic mirror" that reflects the group's activity for the purpose of recognition and empowerment. Indeed, the goal of the transformative method is neither settlement nor productive dialogue but only seeing and choosing.

"Recognition" occurs whenever a group member sees something more clearly than before. This could be the member seeing *his or her own* thoughts, feelings, perceptions, interpretations, body language, actions, values, intentions, challenges, or whatever it might be (e.g., "This issue is very important to me," "I'm feeling discouraged and hopeless," "I'm sighing and rolling my eyes"). It could also be a group member seeing *another member's* thoughts, feelings, and so forth (e.g., "She's silent and tearful," "He's seeing those demands as unreasonable," "She's feeling offended by that suggestion"). Recognition can also involve the members seeing their *group* process more clearly (e.g., "The team is feeling stuck," "We are frequently interrupting each other," "Some of us believe that terminating the meeting would be best").

There is reason for calling the recognition process a *magic* mirror. A principle of quantum physics is the *observer effect,* which refers to changes that the mere act of observation will have on the phenomenon being observed. Simple observation of the use of interventions that promote awareness quickly demonstrates that things often begin to change when they are held in focus— when they are recognized. When IEP team members see themselves and each other more clearly, a change will often quickly follow. It's as if there is a universal principal of human relationships that says

> ## That which is observed changes by virtue of the fact that it is being observed.

Thus, a great deal of the work of the transformative facilitator is to help raise awareness among the group members, knowing that this by itself is a powerful intervention and a key element in an important process. A basic tenet of Gestalt psychology is similar and states that "with awareness comes the ability to make flexible choices." And, in fact, choice through *empowerment* is the other cornerstone of the transformative model.

Empowerment occurs whenever someone is given the opportunity to choose. "You seem to be feeling frustrated" is a reflection to encourage recognition, helping the members to see more clearly an element of their individual or group experience. The next step, according to the transformative method, is highlighting the opportunity for choice. Once members have recognized what they are concerned about, the group or the individual must then decide what to do about it. This is assisted by the facilitator's asking, "Where do you want to go with that?" or simply "What do you want to do now?" This then becomes a moment of choice— of empowerment.

Let's consider some of the many ways in which a group member might respond to such a seemingly simple question. Here are just 10 possibilities from a list of (always) many more:

1. I want an explanation as to why he thinks what I'm asking for is so unreasonable.

2. I want some compassion for my child and recognition of what he can do.

3. I want them to know how difficult it is to even talk to them.

4. I want to just forget it and get out of here.

5. I want to just curl up into a ball and be left alone for a while.

6. I want to talk to the director of special education.

7. I want to know what evidence there is that his idea is a good one.

8. I want to consult with a lawyer.

9. I want to see the specific language of your so-called district policy.

10. I want to file a complaint with the department of education.

See and choose. See and choose. See and choose. This is the opportunity that the transformative facilitator holds out to the group, and the results are often astounding.

JUDGE, GUIDE, AND MIRROR

To more easily remember and distinguish the three models of facilitation, one can think of the evaluative facilitator as a judge, someone who hears both sides of an argument and gives an opinion, although in facilitation the parties can accept or reject it as they wish (unlike in court). The facilitative facilitator, in contrast, is more like a travel guide, offering possibilities for the parties to consider and perhaps sharing information of which the parties might not yet be aware. Yet this guide is only a "hired hand" and would never tell the group what to do or even imply what it *should* do. In contrast, the transformative facilitator is a mirror that reflects what he or she sees and invites the team members to decide for themselves what they want to do next. Table 2.1 summarizes some of the key elements of the three models.

Table 2.1   Philosophies of helping

Evaluative	Facilitative	Transformative
Directive	Supportive	Reflective
Leads	Guides	Follows
Forecasts	Probes/queries with purpose	Asks without direction
Instructs	Proposes "What if . . . ?"	Does not propose
Provides options	Helps generate options	Does not generate options
Powerful, is an authority	Part of the team (for the day)	Powerless
Goal: settlement	Goal: productive dialogue	Goal: recognition and empowerment

COMPARING AND CONTRASTING FACILITATOR STYLES

As may be clear by now, the three facilitator styles are really very different, and it is important to understand both what they look like in practice and what their advantages and disadvantages might be. Let's look now at a few possible situations that might arise in a facilitated IEP meeting and contrast some of the things a facilitator might say. By doing so, one can learn how to "translate" from one style to another in identical circumstances.

An Example of Facilitation Alternatives

Imagine that a facilitator says, "Please remember your ground rules, and let's stay on task." Which style is reflected in this statement? Is this statement more typical of a judge, a travel guide, or a mirror? Well, obviously, by making this statement the facilitator is leading the group and telling the members what they *should* be doing. The statement therefore points very clearly to the evaluative style of the neutral, which is more reminiscent of a judge than a guide or mirror.

What might be a *facilitative* way to express the same good intention—for the group members to stay on task and remember the agreements they made earlier? Think of the "nondirective travel guide" to capture the essence of that style. How about "I'm feeling a little lost. Would it make any sense to review the ground rules you all set—about no interrupting and staying on task?" Here, the facilitator is not directing or telling or judging, only sharing a feeling and then asking an open question. The team members are free to respond with "No, we are doing just fine as it is" (although they probably won't).

How, then, would a transformative facilitator intervene? What would a magic mirror do if the group is interrupting and getting off task? A mirror cannot reflect what it does *not* see, only what is objectively visible to all. Thus, the facilitator would not say, "We are not on task right now" or "You are not following the ground rules." Instead, he or she would focus on what *is* apparent. One easy way to do this is to look at whatever it may have been that led to that perception; for example, "It seems that several people have points they are trying to make." Note that this is an objective statement with which no one could argue, and there is no implication of right or wrong and no implication of what the group should be doing instead. The facilitator has only asked the group to notice (recognize) what is happening. He or she thereby gives the group members an opportunity to choose (empowerment) whether to continue in the same way or to make a change if they want to do something different.

Other chapters, especially Chapters 5 and 6, look more closely at the many options and subtleties that can be involved in the process of reflecting. As just one example, consider the difference between "Several people seem to be speaking at the same time" and "You are constantly interrupting one another, and none of you are listening to what anyone else is trying to say." Both are reflections in identical circumstances, and yet notice the obvious difference in style. Communication occurs on many levels, and it is "not just the words but the music." The facilitator who chooses the latter reflection would be sending a clear message of disapproval and thereby evaluating the group's process. In so doing, he or she would be leading the group (more like a judge than a mirror), and this would be very much outside the realm of the transformative model despite the semblance of a reflection for recognition.

Another Example of Facilitation Alternatives

Imagine that an IEP team is disagreeing about the issue of the "best possible education" for a child. Which style of facilitation is reflected in the following statement: "The law does not require schools to provide the 'best possible education'—only a 'free and appropriate' education"? Is this transformative, facilitative, or directive? By using the judge, guide, and mirror shortcuts to the three styles, the statement is obviously evaluative and directive—the facilitator is telling the group what the "right" answer really is.

How would a facilitative facilitator address this same issue? There is never a single correct answer to such a question, because within any of the models are always many possible choices for what a facilitator might say. One possibility might be simply posing the question and allowing the group to discuss it: "Does the law have any language about the 'best possible education'? Anyone have any ideas about that?" But what if the facilitator already knows the answer to this question? As participant-for-a-day, couldn't he or she save time and be much more helpful by saying, "I am quite certain that the law does discuss this"? Couldn't he or she even go so far as to say, "By way of information, not telling you what to do here, I believe the language of the law is actually 'appropriate education.' Do any of you disagree?" Or could the travel guide be much more gentle and just say, "I seem to recall that there might be some words about this in the law"? If there is such a thing as right- and left-wing facilitative, meaning more or less directive, it seems clear that *some* facilitative interventions lean more in the direction of leading and telling than simply guiding and supporting. It is very important, therefore, to be attentive to the implications of a communication and not just to the words or even the good intention. "Anyone have any ideas?" maximizes the self-direction of the group and minimizes the direction of the facilitator, although all of the options provided fall, theoretically, within the continuum of the facilitative style. More is said about this in later chapters, especially Chapters 5 and 7 in discussing process versus content interventions.

What of the transformative approach? How would a transformative facilitator address this same issue? Once again, the mirror can only reflect what is already there, and the transformative model *only* reflects and invites (recognition and empowerment). One possibility might be "You seem to have differences of opinion about what the law actually says about 'best education.'" This statement could be called *reflecting for recognition*—the mirror is simply holding out for the group to see what is happening. Note that this reflection does not imply right or wrong and does not propose that anything be different. It merely suggests, "Here is what I am seeing."

Consider how different this reflection would be if the same intervention were phrased in different words. Imagine that the facilitator says, "You all seem to be really spinning your wheels now." The perception may be very accurate, and yet notice the twist added by the words *spinning your wheels.* This phrase is value laden and therefore implies that what the team is doing is not right, not acceptable. As soon as such a twist is woven into the facilitator's communication, his or her words are no longer transformative but have become evaluative.

Another subtlety has to do with whether the mirror is following the team or whether it is instead leading. Imagine the facilitator says, "You seem to need help answering this question." The perception may be correct, and yet the facilitator has stepped out of the transformative style and into the directive by suggesting what the team should be doing next (getting help with its question). The facilitator would be less directive and more transformative by simply saying, "This seems to be a hard issue for you right now." The first intervention ("You seem to need help") is a wolf in sheep's clothing and might be considered a veiled attempt at giving information. This is one of the pitfalls that the transformative facilitator must always watch out for. The way to stay safe is to continually remain aware of one's thoughts and feelings and very deliberate in one's choice of words. A good question to always keep in mind here is, "How can I make this more transformative?"

Responding to Questions

How might an evaluative facilitator respond to the following question: "Does the law say anything about who must be present at this meeting?" Evaluative facilitators are often chosen precisely for their expertise. They are *expected* to give information that can fill in the gaps in the team members' understanding.

Therefore, the evaluative facilitator would do his or her best to answer this question and give the information requested. He might say, "Yes, in fact, the law requires that there be a number of people present, including . . . ."

Would a facilitative facilitator respond the same way? After all, wouldn't a travel guide know a lot that could be helpful to the people on the tour bus? Ultimately the facilitative neutral's role is to support the group to do its best work, and the goal of facilitative facilitation is not settlement but productive dialogue. In keeping with this vision, the facilitative facilitator would not answer the question so much as help the group to find its own answers: "That's a good question. Anyone have any thoughts about that?" or "How would it be helpful to have an answer to that question? What would happen next if we knew the answer?" or "Is there anyone you can think of who might know the answer?" Any of these would be squarely in keeping with the facilitative model. In contrast, giving the answer would border on being directive, even if the facilitator is only trying to help.

How would the transformative facilitator respond to such a question? Well, what does the mirror see? "Sounds like you have some questions about the law" or "This seems to be an important issue for you now" or "You are asking whether the law says anything about who must be present" or "I notice some disagreement over this question." All of these statements are objective and free of direction or judgment, and they assist the group members to see what is happening for them, whether on an individual or group level. These answers involve repeating or reflecting for recognition, which is the first half of the transformative process. What about the other half: empowerment?

As mentioned earlier, empowerment takes place whenever someone is given the opportunity to choose. In some ways, it is inherent in recognition. That is, by reflecting the group's or the individual's process, the facilitator automatically provides the opportunity for the group or individual to take the next step. Recognition leads to choice; the two go hand in hand. At the same time, the facilitator could specifically add an empowering piece to the equation by asking the team, "So what do you want to do next?" or "Where would you like to go with that?" Such questions are very much characteristic of the transformative method; by asking them, the facilitator assists the participants to be very conscious and deliberate in their choices.

"What Should We Do?"

What if one of the participants turns to the facilitator and asks very directly, "What should we do?" Obviously, the philosophical model of the facilitator dictates the answer. Can you identify the likely response of the facilitator from each of the evaluative, facilitative, and transformative perspectives?

If we return to the judge–guide–mirror analogy, the judge (evaluative and directive) might answer the question by saying, "Well, in my opinion, I think your best move would be to . . . ." The guide (facilitative) would avoid giving direction but would instead support and encourage productive discussion: "What are your own thoughts about that?" Because option generation *is* permissible along the spectrum of facilitative options, he or she might go a step further and ask, "Well, would it make sense to have an independent evaluation done?" or "What would you think about asking one of the district consultants to observe the child?" But—and this is a big *but*—if the facilitator wanted to stay true to the facilitative model and not cross the line into directive, he or she would emphasize that it is the team that has all wisdom and power. Toward this end, the facilitator might add some qualifiers, such as "I don't know if this idea is of any value, but see what you think" or "It's entirely up to you—just a thought for you to consider." Another big *but* is that skilled facilitative facilitators always recognize that their options fall along a continuum and would choose first to maximize the self-direction of the team, reserving their more active contribution for when the team members cannot do it on their own. As mentioned earlier, this continuum of facilitative options is presented now only as a backdrop against which to compare and contrast the different philosophical approaches. It should be emphasized, however, that some states and agencies are limiting the facilitator's role to process, not content, interventions, as will be further discussed in Chapters 5 and 7.

The transformative model is probably the least familiar to most people. Transformative facilitators see themselves as powerless; they have no attachment to settlement, and they are committed to an impersonal stance, as if thinking, "I am here to follow and reflect; I'm a mirror not a team member." Once again, the mirror cannot reflect what is *not* present. The mirror cannot see "You don't yet have what you need to move forward." All it can see is "You seem to have a question about what you should do" or "You are asking me what you should do." The person espousing this model must be comfortable with tension, because there are often moments of confusion, uncertainty, and possibly even irritation when the facilitator refuses to adopt the role that the participants may be expecting.

IDENTIFYING FACILITATOR STYLES

As an exercise, and for purposes of skill development, participants in facilitation training are asked to take several very directive statements and translate them into both facilitative and transformative styles. Their answers become a springboard for discussion on the path of taking new concepts to the deeper levels of true understanding and then expression through behavior. The following translation exercises may assist you to move through these three stages of mastery (i.e., concept, understanding, and expression) while developing practical skills in the transformative and facilitative methods.

An evaluative facilitator might say, "Before we begin this meeting, let's set a few ground rules." Everyone knows how helpful it can be to have some agreements in place at the start of the meeting, such as being respectful, not interrupting, and so forth. Before reading further, you might like to pause for a moment, take out a pen and a blank sheet of paper, and see if you can guess how a facilitative facilitator might express this same good idea—for the group to establish some proposals that might help their meeting to run more smoothly. Remembering the simple analogy of the travel guide might help. Then, whenever you are ready, read on.

There is no single right answer to the question of what a facilitative facilitator might say, only a range of options that reflect the general principles of the approach. For instance, the facilitative facilitator (i.e., the guide) usually speaks in questions, *asking* if the group might like to consider an idea that could possibly be helpful. To avoid any appearance of telling the team what to do, the guide might use any of a variety of qualifiers so as to tone down the communication and instead accentuate the decision-making power of the group. Qualifiers include such "wishy-washy" words as *possibly, maybe, might, sometimes,* and so forth. Thus, the facilitative facilitator might say something such as "Would it be helpful to maybe set a few guidelines for what might make your meeting run more smoothly, like no interrupting, or being respectful, or staying on task? Is that something that could possibly be worthwhile? What do you all think?"

As another possibility, a facilitative facilitator might say, "Would anyone like to make any proposals for your meeting today—sort of like ground rules—like no interrupting, staying on task, being respectful . . . anything like that? Might that be helpful in any way?" The facilitator *may* participate in option generation; he or she *is* a participant for the day and does bring process expertise. The key here, however, is that any suggestions are offered very gently, leaving the group entirely free to disagree or even say, "No thanks," much as members of a tour group can say, "No thanks," when the tour guide asks if any of them might be interested in visiting an old cathedral.

How would a transformative facilitator handle this same question? Well, the mirror cannot reflect what is not present and thus cannot reflect "I notice that there are no ground rules" any more than "I notice that no one is laughing" or "I notice that no one wore blue." The mirror only sees what is there, and for this reason, technically speaking, the facilitator who is true to the transformative method really cannot intervene at this time. When it comes to recognition and empowerment, there is no move to be made. To get around this challenge, some proponents of the transformative approach make a distinction between the administrative segment of the meeting and the meeting itself. As part of setting the stage *before the meeting begins,* they permit giving information in a form such as the following: "Some people like to make proposals for their meeting, in terms of what they want their meeting to look like, such as no interrupting or being respectful. Is this something any of you would like to do today?" Because this book endorses both transformative *and* facilitative styles, such an approach is considered perfectly acceptable for use in the IEP environment. At the same time, it seems hard to justify such assistance within a *purely* transformative model because it is clearly leading the group, giving information, and indirectly giving advice.

As an exercise, can you translate each statement below into a facilitative and transformative alternative? A great deal of facilitation involves precisely this challenge: taking something one might be thinking and making it more transformative and less directive. Model responses are provided in Appendix A.

Exercises in Facilitator Styles

Translate each of the following into facilitative and transformative styles:

1. None of you is following your own agreed-upon ground rules.

2. You are really upset but keeping it all bottled up inside.

3. You have a really bad attitude.

4. You should at least try to understand them before arguing.

5. This is not going to be settled today.

ADVANTAGES AND DISADVANTAGES TO EACH STYLE

Having briefly explored the three major styles of facilitation, we can now begin to compare and contrast them in terms of their pros and cons. This is a very important exercise because the choice of philosophical model will drive the behavior of the facilitator, and the choice we make will be based on which model we think is best.

Evaluative Pros and Cons

On the positive side, the evaluative facilitator brings the maximum level of new expertise to the meeting. This is especially true if the facilitator is an experienced special education professional and/or an expert in special education law. Because the goal is settlement, there may be a higher probability of the team reaching an agreement and arriving at a signed IEP. Using the directive style will probably enable the facilitator to shorten the meeting, "cutting to the chase" and making sure the group is wasting no time. Lengthy discussion may not be necessary provided the facilitator has the information required for advice and decision. It also is generally unnecessary to consult with people who are not present at the meeting. After all, the facilitator can tell the group what is correct and lawful, what options will or will not work, and how the dispute might play out in a hearing or state complaint investigation. The facilitator can add a great deal to the meeting while preventing wasted time and effort and minimizing confusion and delay.

Yet another possible advantage of the evaluative method is that it is very culturally familiar. Collectively speaking, Americans are comfortable looking to outside experts to settle their disagreements. For the more than 30 years that special education law has been part of the educational arena, groups who have disagreed have had the option to appeal to the state department of education, or to a hearing officer, or to a director of special education, or to a principal or superintendent. Chain of command is inherently authoritative, directive, and evaluative. We know it, and we often use it. When it comes to facilitation, it would be easy to have someone in authority attend the IEP meeting and help make decisions for the benefit of the child. Almost any school district could easily provide someone with the necessary expertise to see a team through its conflict; the resources are already on hand, and it would be an easy transition from administrator one day to facilitator the next—provided the evaluative approach is the one being used.

Are there any downsides to the evaluative method? Well, yes, there are many. There is the issue of dependency. One can generally assume that an IEP team will not request facilitation when team members are getting along *well* and have a thorough understanding of the challenges they face. By relying on a facilitator to get them through their difficulties, how much better prepared will they be to get through their difficulties the *next* time? The team members may learn nothing more than that, whenever they are having trouble, they can always ask a facilitator to come and do it for them.

Another huge downside to the evaluative method has to do with the difference between settlement and resolution. When a judge raps a gavel in a court of law, a conflict may be settled, but is it really resolved? Do the parties leave the courthouse arm in arm, eternally grateful to the judge for restoring peace in the home or workplace or community? Whenever people go to court to have their issues settled, there is sure to be a winner and a loser, or perhaps even two losers; whenever this happens, there are sure to be bad feelings. Nobody likes to be on the losing side. If parent and school are arguing about the most appropriate services for the child, or if the general classroom teacher and the special education teacher are at odds, or if the staff and the administrator disagree—in any of these scenarios, the risk is very great that the facilitator's supporting one side over the other will leave the opposing side feeling left out and unhappy. Yes, there may be a signed agreement at the end of the meeting, but is harmony restored within the team?

Finally, quicker and easier are not always best. Whenever a group of people are working together toward consensus, there will always be a variety of perspectives to consider and to integrate into the final product. It is as if each member brings one piece of a puzzle to the table, and all of the pieces must be in place for the most complete picture to emerge. This ensures not only that all members will be satisfied with the outcome but also that all points of view are included for the benefit of the child. Including the thoughts of all group members is much more likely to happen with the facilitative and transformative models than with the evaluative approach.

Facilitative Pros and Cons

The facilitative model has a number of features in common with the evaluative model. Americans have a cultural familiarity with the facilitative approach. That is, collectively speaking, we are familiar with a *number* of people who can be impartial and supportive of a team that is having difficulty (e.g., counselors, ombudsmen, liaisons, mediators). If policy allows, the facilitative neutral *can* add to the expertise of the group by assisting with option generation (e.g., "Have you considered doing . . . ?" or "Would it make sense to try . . . ?"). He or she can also supplement the expertise of the group by giving information, provided there is no implication of what should or should not be done, or what is right or wrong. For reasons that will be explained in Chapter 5, this is a slippery slope best avoided, and yet it is still theoretically within the facilitative model. The facilitative facilitator can also help the group to watch the time and stay on task, to set and honor ground rules, and to maintain respect and courtesy. In contrast to the evaluative approach, however, the facilitative facilitator does this by asking or by very gently proposing something for the group's consideration rather than by leading or directing.

The facilitative model also offers some advantages that are not offered by the evaluative approach. One is a commitment to drawing on the expertise *of the group* rather than the facilitator himself or herself. The facilitative facilitator's expertise is not so much in clarifying special education facts as in clarifying pathways to meaningful discussion. Thus, the facilitator asks questions that help the group to pool its own resources, clarify its own wisdom, and generate its own options, thereby making synergy possible.

Synergy is a wonderful concept that is, in a sense, a mathematical impossibility. By definition, it means that the sum of the whole is greater than its parts. Thus, if three people are working together, the power they have is not $1 + 1 + 1 = 3$ but rather 4 or even more! This enormous potential of groups to achieve more than the individuals can achieve by themselves is demonstrated again and again in collaborative venues such as mediation and counseling. Whenever people are supported to communicate effectively and to work *together* toward the achievement of their common goals, synergy will usually emerge. It is often surprising and at times amazing, and yet also the very realistic potential of every group. The facilitative model, with its emphasis on productive dialogue, is one such venue in which teams can be helped to achieve their synergistic potential.

Another benefit is that the facilitative facilitator helps to safeguard the collaborative process and to ensure that all participants have a chance to speak and be heard. The facilitator can help maintain a level playing field so that everyone feels welcome to participate and so that the meeting is not dominated by the more outspoken or commanding members.

Above all, the facilitative facilitator, in contrast to the evaluative facilitator, brings what has been called *process expertise* (as opposed to content expertise). In this regard, he or she knows how to help the team communicate more effectively and handle such feelings as discouragement, anger, hopelessness, and injustice. Such support promotes the possibility of true resolution, which may not occur if settlement is the only goal or outcome. Through facilitative interventions, the team members may also learn to express themselves in ways that, in future meetings, will be more productive than simply out-shouting one another, walking away mad, or terminating the meeting prematurely when hope and progress are still very much possible.

Given these many benefits, are there no downsides to the facilitative model? Well, the facilitative model is inherently a collaborative one, and collaboration takes *time*. The facilitative model may not be as quick or as easy as the directive approach because it provides an opportunity for the team to move in directions other than simply determining what is right and wrong in the development of the IEP. Instead, members will be encouraged to hear all sides and consider all perspectives, to verbalize feelings, to articulate intentions and expectations, and to be more conscious and deliberate in all that they decide. This is not always a comfortable route and not always a familiar one, and it may not fit with the expectations of those who have requested facilitation.

Furthermore, depending on the setting, a pool of facilitators who can effectively use the facilitative approach may not be readily available. Filling this gap may require training would-be facilitators (and to some extent all participants) in a new way of thinking about conflict and disagreement—not as something to be avoided or suppressed but as something to be honored and supported so that the team members can explore their different perspectives and incorporate them into an even greater whole. Only in this way can true collaboration take place and true synergy emerge. This training may involve time and expense, or it may involve the expense of hiring outside neutrals who already have the necessary skills.

Another possible downside to the facilitative model is that not all school professionals can easily switch hats and take on the role of an unbiased third party. A common concern among those receiving training in this model is, "Wow, it's hard to stop being an administrator and just support their process, especially when you know that some of what they're saying is not true, and when they're so used to seeing me as someone they can turn to who can answer their questions."

And what of that question of dependency? Will the group be strengthened and its team spirit restored if, whenever there are disagreements or hard feelings, team members must call on an outside party to help them do their work? After all, the group will probably be meeting again and again in the future to plan for the child's education. Will the team members know how to do this more effectively if the facilitator does a great deal of their work? That is, if the facilitator sets the ground rules, keeps the group on task, ensures a level playing field, probes for members' feelings and good intentions, and so forth, will the group members know how to do all this for themselves the next time they meet?

Transformative Pros and Cons

The transformative model is easy to approach from the negative. It takes time. It is culturally unfamiliar. It may fail to satisfy the expectations of the group. It may be difficult to find facilitators who are skilled in its use. It may invite considerable doubt and resistance from those who have not yet seen its potential. It is a difficult hat to wear for those who are comfortable in a position of expertise and authority. It is also a difficult role to play for those who feel an overwhelming desire to be helpful; it requires patience and a willingness to let the tensions be, and a willingness to let the team find its own strength rather than rush to supply it for them. It requires the discipline to wait for the right time to intervene as well as the good judgment to know when to remain quiet. It also requires letting go of any attachment to whether the group settles its differences and comes into consensus, instead being attached only to a process that may not always go where one hopes for it to go.

Yet despite all these downsides, there are many pros. The transformative model gets its name from the promise of "transformation." That is, it is called *transformative* because of its potential to change relationships. Of the three approaches to facilitation, it maximizes the potential of the group to see its own process—to recognize its own values, assumptions, beliefs, expectations, intentions, goals, wisdom, and needs. It promotes no winners and losers, only choosers—only clear opportunities for self-direction, both individually and collectively.

For these reasons, the transformative method maximizes the potential for growth and then independence among the group members. It does not take group members long to anticipate what the facilitator is likely to say or not to say. Before long they will be asking themselves, "What am I feeling? What am I saying with my body language? What is it I want? How are we interacting right now? What do I want to do next? What do we as a team want to do?" Of the three methods, it is the transformative that most ensures that the group members will interact more effectively when the facilitator is no longer there. In this is its transformative power.

Another advantage is that it is easy, almost lazy, work—the main task for the facilitator is careful listening, and the list of intervention options is really very short (as will be clarified in Chapter 5). The facilitator must listen very attentively, knowing when to *stay out* of it—when to let the group continue on its course—and when to speak up and hold out a reflection or an opportunity for choice. The greatest advantage of all is that this process works, and it works extremely well. It is so remarkably powerful that it deserves to be called a *magic* mirror. But only experience will prove this to the newcomer. People have to see it to believe it, and yet, golden guaranteed, they will.

As an aside, I have been a contract mediator for the U.S. Postal Service for more than 10 years through its REDRESS (Resolve Employment Disputes, Reach Equitable Solutions Swiftly) Program for discrimination complaints. Most employee disputes are handled in house, but discrimination complaints involve the use of independent neutrals who are not employees of the Postal Service. Prior to and concurrent with this experience, I have worked in the courts with lawyers, judges, and litigants and also as a counselor and a mediator in private practice. From these three pathways, I have had a chance to see all three methods of facilitation in action. Evaluative and directive styles are most commonly used among lawyers and judges in connection with court mediation. The facilitative style is the one to which counselors and therapists seem to naturally gravitate. The transformative method is actually *required* by the Postal Service, whose administrators reserve the right to observe their mediators at work, and they can at any time choose to correct a mediator or strike him or her from the roster for failing to use the transformative model.

The majority of Postal Service mediator applicants come from backgrounds in court or community mediation, counseling, psychology, and social work.

They often show great resistance to the transformative method and express considerable doubt that such a model can be effective. This *same* resistance and doubt is common among school personnel in training to become facilitators of IEP meetings. Yet by being forced to use the transformative method and to continually enhance their skills at using it, many Postal Service mediators come to find that it really is a surprisingly powerful and effective means of helping people reach consensus. There is, however, one significant downside: It limits the "range of motion" of the mediator. In other words, there may be things one cannot say because policy prohibits it as not being transformative. In a strict interpretation of the model, the facilitator may not assist with option generation, may not give information, and may not take a more active and supportive role when the participants are unresponsive to transformative interventions alone—options that *are* possible within the facilitative and evaluative models. Much more is said about this in later chapters, especially Chapter 5.

CONCLUSIONS

Given the many downsides of the evaluative method, it is my belief that this philosophy of intervention has no place in IEP facilitation. It can too easily fan the fires of adversity, and even when it does result in settlement, it can too easily leave unresolved feelings that will come back to haunt the team in other ways and at future meetings. If outside expertise or direction is needed, the facilitator can encourage the team members to look to the appropriate professionals who can fulfill this role and provide the leadership, advice, and authority they require. Otherwise, the unique position of the facilitator will be weakened, the potential of the process will be diluted, and the team will not maximize its independence for the future (see Table 2.2).

Instead of being evaluative or directive, IEP facilitators are urged to remain true to the facilitative and transformative methods, but not in that order. The simple recommendation is to strengthen the team to the fullest extent possible

Table 2.2 Recommendation

	Facilitative	Transformative
Avoid evaluative and directive methods.	Supportive	Reflective
	Guides	Follows
	Probes/queries with purpose	Asks without direction
Let *others* provide advice and authority.	Proposes "what if. . . ?"	Does not propose
	Helps generate options	Does not generate options
	A part of the team (today)	Powerless
	Goal: productive dialogue	Recognition and empowerment

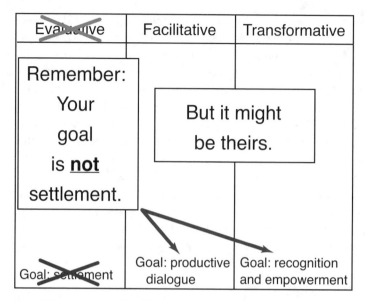

Figure 2.1.   Remember: Your goal is not settlement!

through the recognition and empowerment that come with the transformative style. But the facilitator does not have to be tied to such a limited range of options. He or she can use facilitative interventions when required and yet should do so only when the team cannot do it on its own. Remember: The goal of the facilitative and transformative models is not settlement, although this might be the goal of the team; the role of the facilitator is to help the team achieve *its* goals (see Figure 2.1).

At this early stage, this simple exhortation to *be as transformative as possible and only be facilitative when the team cannot do it on its own* may not seem very clear or helpful. The chapters that follow examine in detail what this means in practice and provide concrete examples that illustrate not just how this can be done but how it can be done very easily.

3 The Ten Roles of the Facilitator

Having discussed the three basic philosophies of how a facilitator goes about helping teams to succeed, let's now turn to the specific roles that he or she plays during individualized education program (IEP) meetings. The style reveals *how* to do it, but *what* exactly is the facilitator trying to do? As explained in Chapter 2, the facilitative approach guides the group toward productive dialogue, whereas the transformative style promotes recognition and empowerment. And yet, does stating these goals in such simple terms offer sufficient practical direction? Is it enough to enable someone to facilitate?

One who follows the facilitative model could theoretically guide the group in any direction at all: "Would it make sense, before we get started, to maybe take just a few moments to talk about chocolate chips . . . or not?" "Team, some groups like to spend a little time talking about weather or sports, or speaking evil about people we know; is this something you all might like to do today?" "Team, does the law have any language about handling citrus fruits without proof of ownership?" The same applies to the transformative facilitator; he or she could theoretically mirror anything and everything: "I notice that some of you are taller than others." "I see that some of you are wearing sneakers; where would you like to go with that?" Obviously, this is the stuff of spoof and comedy, but why? What makes such interventions inappropriate, and, more importantly, what interventions *are* appropriate? This is actually an essential discussion to have, because just having a facilitator present does not ensure success. There is good facilitation and poor facilitation, and which is which depends to a great extent on the intervention points identified by the facilitator—*when* he or she decides is the right time to intervene, or not. A facilitator can only make such decisions wisely when there is considerable clarity about his or her *roles,* apart from the style and the goals of the intervention. In practice, the facilitator may have up to 10 distinct yet interrelated roles, and in this chapter each is explored in detail along with concrete examples.

Ten Roles of the Facilitator

1. Helping all parties feel welcome
2. Helping with ground rules and agenda
3. Setting a good example
4. Safeguarding a collaborative process
5. Promoting positive communication
6. Helping explore interests
7. Helping ensure that all are "on the same page"
8. Clarifying areas of agreement
9. Addressing unproductive communication styles
10. Helping to bring meaningful closure

HELPING ALL PARTIES FEEL WELCOME

When people enter the meeting room, they are sure to make assumptions and carry fears and expectations about the newcomer—the facilitator. A smiling face and a warm handshake can do much to help them feel at ease. A facilitator is unlikely to be called in to assist a group that is getting along well, and therefore he or she should expect, perhaps, to walk into a room already brimming with tensions, mistrust, anxiety, and even hostility. For this reason, the friendly and confident presence that the facilitator brings can begin early on to soften the hard edges.

Prior to the meeting, it is essential that the facilitator make contact—usually by phone—with both the chairperson and the parent. It must never be the case that the facilitator's attendance be a surprise to either of these key figures at the table. By making contact in advance, some of the groundwork for helping the parties feel welcome will already have been done. This usually goes far toward helping to promote a more congenial atmosphere when the members arrive at the meeting. In contrast, if the parents or chairperson appear for the meeting and find that a facilitator has been invited without their prior knowledge and consent, tensions, resistance, and mistrust are very likely to escalate. This preconferencing by phone with both the chairperson and the parent is discussed in further detail in Chapter 4.

In contacting the chairperson prior to the meeting, the facilitator will encourage him or her to have a written agenda and to propose ground rules. The chairperson will also be encouraged to ensure that introductions are made at the start of the meeting and that a facilitation agreement form is signed by all participants (see Appendix K). If, for whatever reason, any element of this stage setting is not done—or not done well—the facilitator will have to be prepared to add some support if necessary.

As a rule, the facilitator should be a keen observer and should generally remain quiet, allowing the chairperson every reasonable opportunity to be the leader of his or her team. The facilitator has to have a good sense of timing as to when to intervene and when to simply listen attentively and be patient. Otherwise, he or she risks being a nuisance, getting in the way, and usurping the chairperson's role as the leader of the meeting. This is one of many reasons why preconferencing with the chairperson by phone is so essential—to minimize the need for the facilitator to intervene.

When people attend meetings and do not know the other participants, they often feel a certain uneasiness and may be distracted by such thoughts as "Why is he here?" "Who is she? Is she the teacher my child was complaining about?" "I've never seen him before; is he even a member of this committee?" "Is she maybe an administrator sent to make sure I don't get out of hand?" People have a tendency to fill in the unknowns with negative rather than positive assumptions, and the facilitator can help to minimize this probability by "pinch hitting" for the chairperson if the ball of making introductions should get dropped. However, the facilitator must give the chairperson a chance; it may be that the chairperson has every intention of making introductions, just at a different moment than the facilitator might have imagined.

Let's talk now about what to do if it is clear that the chairperson has, in fact, neglected this important step in helping the team feel welcome. The facilitator might say something such as, "Excuse me, just a moment. I haven't had the pleasure of meeting all of you. Would it be okay if we take a moment to go around the table and just say our names and what you do in terms of Sarah's education? Would that be okay with you?" Notice the use of lots of questions rather than statements that might appear more directive. Note also the positive and courteous style and the emphasis that the power rests with the team, not the facilitator ("Would that be okay with you?").

Here are some things *not* to do (see also the summary of facilitator dos and don'ts in Appendix B):

1. Do not ignore it. If the group starts the meeting without introductions, tensions are likely to reside under the surface. Tensions are cumulative; they build on one another and raise the probability that more overt conflict will follow.

2. Do not intervene too soon without giving the chairperson a reasonable opportunity to ask the group members to introduce themselves.

3. Do not become directive and "steal the thunder" of the chairperson. For example, do *not* say, "Team, I notice you haven't done any introductions. Let's take a moment now to be sure we all know one another."

4. Do not phrase questions in the negative, for example by saying, "Don't you think we should take a moment for introductions?" Asking questions in the negative is inherently directive because it implies that there is a right answer and that what the team has been doing up to now is not correct.

Again, the facilitator should seize this important intervention point by asking questions that very gently support the team members to *recognize* that they may not yet all know one another and to *empower* them to choose whether it might be helpful to take a moment to share their names and their roles in the education of the child. Having the chairperson read the statement of agreement and circulate it for signatures will help to clarify the role of the facilitator and ensure that all are in agreement.

HELPING WITH GROUND RULES AND AGENDA

Ground rules are an essential part of good meeting management, all the more so when tensions are high and conflict is likely. If the words *ground rules* seem heavy handed or authoritative, some equally valuable alternatives are *guidelines, proposals,* or *agreements*—all of which have to do with how the group wants to conduct its meeting.

It is important to recognize that not all participants will have a thorough understanding of what it means to set ground rules or what particular ground rules might be appropriate or helpful. Very often, unless further guidance is offered, team members will give a quick *no* to the question of whether they might like to make some agreements as to how the meeting should run. This answer will often reflect the team's lack of awareness rather than any careful consideration. An analogy might be the waiter who asks if anyone would like to try the *frabo zhu xhangui* (not a real dish, in all probability). Most are likely to say, "No thank you," rather than even ask what in heaven's name this is. What is easy and what is best are not always the same, and wisdom clearly dictates having ground rules—and having them in place before tensions get out of hand rather than after.

Ground rules serve two invaluable purposes. First, they provide direction through a clear and shared set of expectations. Because people tend to comply with what they freely agree to do, the team's making agreements to be respectful, to not interrupt, to turn off cell phones, and so forth, are *by themselves* likely to reduce the probability that those issues will surface during the meeting. And because team members have agreed to these ground rules, all it often takes to restore "law and order" is a gentle reminder in the form of simply asking how the team members are doing with their ground rules. Thus, as a second benefit, ground rules serve as a safety net on which the group can easily fall back should it become necessary. Consider the alternative: Without ground rules, there is no prevention through agreement, and there is no fall-back plan because there is nothing in place to fall back on—one can't remind a group about their ground rules if there were never any set to begin with. Experience has shown again and again how valuable such agreements are to a harmonious meeting, and yet because the participants may not have used them before and seen their benefits, they may quickly say, "No, thanks," to this soup *du jour* that they really should try.

Yet another consideration with regard to ground rules has to do with assumptions and expectations. People come to meetings with unspoken beliefs about what is fair and appropriate, and if these are never openly discussed, the probability is very high that the team members will have very different sets of expectations. Thus, an administrator may consider it absolutely fine to talk on his cell phone—after all, he is responsible for many children and can easily multitask without having to step out of the meeting. A teacher might believe that leaving the meeting to check on her classroom is her professional responsibility, given all of the other children she is leaving behind. An advocate may feel that taking control of the meeting at times helps level the playing field and empower the parent. Yet when any of these good intentions are expressed in action, they can easily lead to ill will and adverse reactions among those who do not necessarily agree with the behaviors, even when they share the underlying values (i.e., being responsible, caring for children, and ensuring a level playing field). How much better it would be if such proposals were verbalized, clarified, and agreed upon. This is a clear example of the process of recognition and empowerment—the team members can become aware of their values (recognition) and then decide together (empowerment) how best to manage them and proceed with their meeting. This cannot happen if people simply sit down and start talking with no such agreements in place.

Given that the facilitator is not an authority of any kind, how can he or she help with setting ground rules? Well, as mentioned previously, the facilitator can preconference with the chairperson and encourage him or her to be sure to set ground rules. This may warrant some instruction, because the chairperson may not yet have learned about this facet of meeting management. Consider also that the facilitator is not a facilitator on the phone. At this early stage, the facilitator can enter into an advisory or instructional role that will not be an option during the meeting—all the more reason to take full advantage in the preconferencing stage.

On the phone in advance of the meeting, the facilitator can encourage the chairperson to set ground rules at the start of the meeting. However, it is important that these be a product of the group rather than an imposition of the chair. Otherwise the group will not have the "ownership" necessary to ensure goodwill and compliance. For this reason, the chairperson should be encouraged to *propose* ground rules and ask for agreement, rather than tell the group what the ground rules will be and just assume that the group will accept and abide by them. "Asking is affirming" is a saying that speaks to an essential element of group process: Asking questions communicates welcoming, respect, inclusion, and interest and signifies that what the participants have to share is of value. Speaking in questions rather than statements is thus an important feature of diplomacy, collaboration, conflict resolution, facilitation, and so many facets of effective meeting management and interpersonal skill.

What then would be some appropriate ground rules for a team to consider? There are usually just a handful. Again, it must be emphasized that these must be *proposed* to the team with an invitation to agree and not presented as a done deal with the expectation of compliance.

Sample Ground Rules

1. Remember the purpose: to serve the child.
2. Make good use of time.
3. Stay on task and avoid side talking.
4. Be courteous and respectful.
5. Turn off cell phones.
6. Remain together until breaks.
7. Speak up if someone has an "owie."

Although most of the items on the list of sample ground rules are self-evident, the final one warrants some explanation. The "owie rule" is a proposal that, if someone should at any time feel troubled or upset by something that is said, that person will speak up and let it be known so that the group can respond and help resolve the issue or concern. The alternative would be to let those troubled feelings be an obstacle for the remainder of the meeting, possibly festering and growing to the point that the possibility of meaningful discussion, positive team spirit, and a successful meeting outcome could be greatly diminished.

Even if the facilitator talks about ground rules with the chairperson beforehand by phone, what if this ball still gets dropped and the meeting is started without them—or without the participants *mutually agreeing* to them? This then is another intervention point at which the facilitator has to be prepared to pinch hit. The recommendations for how to do so are very similar to those discussed previously with regard to introductions. For example, the facilitator might say, "May I just ask a question? I'm sorry to interrupt. Some groups have found it helpful to have some agreements at the start of their meetings, such as no interrupting, or being respectful, or turning off cell phones. Is this something any of you might want to do today? Might that be helpful at all?" Notice once again the use of questions and an emphasis that power rests with the team, not the facilitator.

The following are some don'ts:

1. Do not ignore it.

2. Do not intervene too soon without giving the chairperson a reasonable opportunity to suggest establishing ground rules.

3. Do not become directive, for example, by saying, "Team, I notice that you haven't set any ground rules. Shouldn't we set a few as a safeguard for the meeting?" or "There are no ground rules in place. Does anyone think we ought to set some?" Remember that a mirror cannot reflect what is *not* seen and that to ask questions in the negative implies a judgment of right and wrong, of should and should not.

There are two final issues of importance with regard to helping the meeting get started on a positive note: agendas and time projections. In this first regard, the team will benefit greatly by having a written agenda that is visible to all participants (see Appendix C). After all, the agreement to stay on task is difficult to follow if the team does not know what "on task" really means. A written agenda provides a very helpful support in this regard.

The agenda is another issue that would typically be discussed with the chairperson prior to the meeting. If for any reason the chairperson takes no steps in proposing an agenda, the facilitator might intervene by saying something like, "May I just ask, is this an initial referral or a 3-year review? Or what kind of IEP meeting is this one? Would it make sense to outline some of the key segments of your meeting so we're all clear on what has been covered and what still lies ahead?" Given that this will have been discussed over the phone with the chairperson in advance, it is sure to serve more as a reminder to the chairperson rather than as unexpected news. It should therefore be a very easy omission to correct.

The second key issue to address is time projections, whether anyone will be leaving early. Are all members prepared to stay for the entire meeting? If someone has to leave, will that person be coming back? If someone cannot stay, do the members understand the reason for this so they will avoid making negative assumptions (e.g., "He doesn't care," "She's so inconsiderate," "My child is not important," "How very unprofessional"). If someone *must* leave early, knowing this in advance can help the team be sure to discuss the topics most relevant to that member early on, rather than have that person rushing out the door or gone altogether when his or her input is particularly needed. Also, if the person who must leave is a legally required participant in the meeting, the team will benefit from having sufficient notice to find a replacement so that the meeting would not need to be suddenly terminated or would risk being out of compliance with the law if it were to continue without that required member. All too often, IEP meetings begin without ever addressing this critical issue of leaving early, usually because the participants have not yet been trained in how important it is and how easily it can be handled. In his or her preconference with the chairperson, therefore, the facilitator should encourage him or her to ask members whether they are able to stay for the entire meeting. Thus, the chairperson will probably address this, but if not, the facilitator can be ready to serve as the backup.

The dos and don'ts are similar to those discussed previously. The facilitator should watch for it. If the chairperson does not raise the issue of leaving early, the facilitator can ask, "Just so we are all on the same page, does anyone have an idea about how long this meeting is likely to last? I know we can never predict for sure." When the members say 1, 2, or more hours, the facilitator can then ask, "Is everyone free to stay for that time? Would anyone have to leave before then?" If the teacher says he has to return to his classroom at 1:15, or the principal says she has another meeting at 1:30, then the group is less likely to demonize (interpret negatively) when those people do in fact leave. The group can also make decisions about how best to address these unexpected developments. Once again, the facilitator has assisted the team members with recognition of their situation and empowerment in choosing how they wish to proceed.

The don'ts include the following:

1. Do not ignore it.

2. Do not intervene too soon without giving the chairperson a reasonable opportunity to raise the question of the probable length of the meeting and the issue of people having to leave early.

SETTING A GOOD EXAMPLE

Although setting a good example may seem to warrant no explanation at all, some features and implications may not be obvious. What *is* perhaps obvious is that the facilitator must be pleasant, positive, courteous, calm, respectful, diplomatic, and so forth. But does everyone really know how to do that? No matter how skilled a person might be, chances are that he or she can learn still more in this regard, so it is helpful to approach this set of skills as dynamic rather than fixed. Although one can learn to bake cookies in an hour or so, becoming a gourmet baker may take many years.

Similarly, certain essential facilitator skills cannot be mastered in a day, or from a book, or even from any number of sessions gaining experience as a facilitator. Instead, some skills are as much art as science, and facilitators are always challenged by the new and unexpected as they work with unique individuals and their unique circumstances. For this reason, part of the good example set by a facilitator is to be humble, open to growth, careful about making assumptions, and willing to be wrong. Participants may not be able to articulate exactly how a facilitator shows this (or even that the facilitator is showing this) and yet may sense his or her open and receptive attitude as a stabilizing presence in their group process. It has been said that "attitude is everything," and the skilled facilitator has a positive attitude, an open mind and heart, and a true willingness to learn.

The skilled facilitator is also a keen observer and is very aware not just of the group but also of himself or herself. This awareness has to do with body postures, tones of voice, and similar unspoken communications. It also has to do with word choices and the general principles of tact and diplomacy. Also required is a high level of sensitivity, listening not only with the ears but also, in a sense, with the heart, so as to remain very much tuned in to how the group members are really feeling, beyond whatever it is they may be saying.

An important part of self-awareness for the facilitator relates to his or her personal goals at the meeting. If the facilitator wants to see agreement, he or she runs a greater risk of becoming directive. If instead the facilitator can remain true to the transformative and facilitative models recommended here, then the example he or she sets will be one of constantly looking for opportunities for recognition, empowerment, and productive dialogue. It will not take long before the group members begin to catch on and learn from the facilitator's example that there is a certain attitude of openness and respect—and a few key questions and comments—that tend to promote their progress.

People seem to have a certain amount of a herd instinct in that tension in one person tends to foster more tension in the group, and calmness tends to promote the same. The facilitator therefore does well to pay close attention to the energy he or she is adding to the mix at the table. Remaining physically relaxed promotes a similar calmness in others, and listening attentively is likely to encourage others to do the same. An interesting feature of facilitation is that one can easily wonder what the same meeting might have been like had no facilitator been present. Perhaps the mere presence of a positive, relaxed, and respectful participant at the table is a balancing and positive influence on the team. And the facilitator must also be an optimist—one who trusts with an unshakeable faith that people can and will do great things if simply given the opportunity to work together collaboratively.

SAFEGUARDING A COLLABORATIVE PROCESS

Safeguarding a collaborative process is ultimately the *only* role of the facilitator. Everything else being presented and discussed is really just one or another means of supporting the team's collaboration. It is as if the facilitator's real purpose is to offer bridge after bridge across whatever it may be that is keeping the team members apart or would threaten to do so if not effectively addressed. Although the following list may not be absolutely comprehensive, these seven factors, which were presented in Chapter 1, support the collaborative process in general.

Keys to Collaboration

1. Remembering the common purpose

2. Giving everyone a voice

3. Communicating openly yet with respect

4. Assuming good reason and intention

5. Exploring underlying interests

6. Valuing the team and its members

7. Trusting the process

Don't the roles of the facilitator that we have previously discussed merely serve to support team collaboration? Helping everyone feel welcome helps the team members feel valued. Helping ensure that an agenda and ground rules are in place helps the participants communicate more effectively. Setting a good example means trusting the process and demonstrating the characteristics of a *collaborative* member, one who listens with respect, communicates well, remembers the purpose, and so forth. And yet the facilitator must do more than *just* set a good example: He or she has the unique responsibility of helping the others maintain a collaborative process—something they may not yet know how to do very well. He or she must therefore bring a box of collaborative tools and know when and how to use them to build bridges as the need arises. Let's turn now to explore what this will look like in practice.

Ultimately, collaboration is a process of sharing, and the facilitator must be ever alert to whether sharing is in fact taking place. When it is not, it is time to intervene. Thus, as long as the team is sharing ideas, communicating constructively, engaging in their process, and making progress, there really is *nothing* for the facilitator to do except continue to listen attentively, observe carefully, and be prepared to intervene when it becomes necessary.

An analogy worth considering is the cuckoo clock. Who would buy one if not for the little birdie that comes out and makes a lovely sound every once in a while? But who would buy one if it was *always* cuckooing, and not just when necessary to tell the time? Analogies aside, the reality is that most cuckoos in most cuckoo clocks come out only twice an hour—once to toll the hour and once to chirp the half. Returning to facilitation, it is impossible to quantify the rate of intervention of a good facilitator or a bad one. The appropriate rate of intervention has everything to do with how much the particular group requires it. I'm proud to say that I once facilitated a 2-hour IEP meeting in which I never intervened at all! After introducing myself as the facilitator in the opening remarks, I said not a word for the next 2 hours. The reason was simple: There was no need to intervene because the group was collaborating extremely well. Other meetings have warranted more active participation, but as a general rule, little is good. The greater rule is this: Intervene when necessary; otherwise, don't. What makes intervention necessary, of course, is when collaboration is not taking place, and what makes it unnecessary is when the group is doing fine on its own. Thus, as long as empowerment, recognition, and meaningful dialogue *are* taking place, a very quiet facilitator is probably doing *great* work.

What of those instances when collaboration is *not* happening? How would the facilitator know? What might be the symptoms? The obvious ones are the breaking of ground rules, raised voices, passivity and withdrawal, unhappy faces, belligerent tones, unproductive discussion, and so forth. Simply stating the converse of the seven keys to collaboration points directly to the intervention points for facilitation.

What Impairs Collaboration?

1. Losing sight of the common purpose
2. Some members having no voice
3. Communicating poorly and without respect
4. Engaging in demonizing and accusation
5. Focusing on competing positions
6. Discounting the team and its members
7. Losing faith in the process

Most of these require no explanation, and yet a few illustrations might round out a sense of what each of these can look like in practice. These can be considered critical junctures for intervention because, if not addressed, tensions are likely to escalate and the team is unlikely to achieve its goals.

Losing Sight of the Common Purpose

Instead of focusing on the current tasks, the team members may be talking about things in the past or future that have little relevance to their agenda. A great deal of time may be spent discussing topics that either do not relate to this day's educational planning for the student or *do relate* but in a way that is not clear. The latter is actually often the case, and the facilitator can assist the group to see how the *apparent* sidetrack really is relevant, perhaps by reflecting to the speaker, "This issue seems very important to you, Mr. Jones, and you must have good reasons for feeling this way." By assuming good reason and intention (another element that promotes collaboration), the facilitator increases the probability that the good intention will be brought out in the open. Mr. Jones might reply, "Well, it *is* important. Johnny's interest in football camp shows that he can plan for the future, that he has lots of energy for things that interest him, and that he may just be learning by his own different path." Or perhaps Mr. Jones will realize that he is in fact off trail: "Well, I guess what happened in Mrs. Mortimer's class last year isn't really relevant to what we're working on right now." The facilitation here involves little more than recognition and empowerment—awareness and then choice.

Some Members Having No Voice

Perhaps only one or two members are doing most of the talking while the other members are showing signs of distress, anxiety, or withdrawal. A common tendency of the beginning facilitator is to mirror what he or she does not see: "I notice that not everyone is sharing." Doesn't this imply that the group is not doing something right? If not everyone is sharing, then the team must not be following *somebody's* rule, and in phrasing the intervention in this way, the facilitator (despite the best of intentions) has crossed into an evaluative and directive role. Yet because the mirror can reflect what *is* present, the facilitator could choose a different way to reflect the same observation: "I notice that some members have been very quiet." Other possibilities might be to simply ask the team, "How are you feeling about your meeting so far?" or "Is everyone feeling comfortable that they have had a chance to speak and be heard?"

Communicating Poorly and without Respect

The facilitator cannot reflect that the group members are communicating "poorly" or "without respect" without making a very obvious evaluation of their process. What then could be done to remain more true to the transformative or facilitative models? Well, whenever the facilitator feels tempted to intervene, it will always be because something has happened to give the impression that such an intervention is warranted. Objectively speaking, then, what would that be? The facilitator can always silently wonder, "What is it that leads me to see this as poor?" Perhaps it is frequent interruptions ("I notice that there are several conversations going on at the same time"). Perhaps it is raised voices ("There seem to be some strong feelings right now"). Maybe it is crossed arms and rolling eyes ("I sense some dissatisfactions in the room"). In other words, whatever it is can be held up for all to see in an objective manner that helps the team members be aware (recognition) and yet leaves them free to either make a change or continue the same way (choice/empowerment).

Another more facilitative intervention that is often applicable is to simply ask the team, "How are you all feeling about your meeting at this point?" This technique could be called *pause for reflection.* Although the facilitator asks the group members to be aware of their feelings and to recognize their group process, he or she leads rather than follows, which more closely characterizes the guide than the mirror (i.e., is more facilitative than transformative). More on faulty communications among the team members is said later in this chapter and in the chapters ahead.

Engaging in Demonizing and Accusation

Demonizing and accusations are to be expected whenever people are in an unresolved conflict. *Demonizing* refers to the tendency to attribute global negative perceptions about another person, far beyond whatever behavior or statement may have been found objectionable by the "opponent." Thus, someone who feels hurt when someone else seems to imply that her idea is unrealistic may see that person as an "egomaniac" who "doesn't care about anyone's opinions but his own" and who has "about as much tact as a corn cob." *Global,* in this context, means broad and all-encompassing, and demonizing is just this way—it involves making sweeping generalizations that apply to the person as a whole rather than to a very specific belief, statement, or behavior. It also tends to involve a completely one-sided perception, as if the opponent is wholly to blame and the demonizer has had no role in or contribution to the conflict or misunderstanding at all. Demonizing seems to be a normal human tendency but one that is of limited value for mutual understanding, healing, growth, and progress.

What then can the skilled facilitator do about demonizing and accusations, or should any intervention even be made? After all, it is *their* process, their meeting, their discussion. Why not just let it be and wait to see if anyone else feels inclined to address it? The answer to such questions begins with the recognition that demonizing and accusations undermine collaboration. So long as I see the other person as a wicked and malicious enemy, how can I possibly listen with respect and communicate in the positive manner that ensures the forward progress of the team? Chances are that I cannot, and this demonizing will of necessity be a serious obstacle to collaboration. It is a critical juncture for intervention because the team is not collaborating if its members are demonizing. Also consider that "owies" (emotional reactions) are cumulative—they fester and grow and build on each other until, eventually, they find expression, often in explosion. Thus, if someone is sitting on a powder keg of negativity, this is also obstructing collaboration—that is, working together toward common objectives. It, too, becomes a juncture for intervention because collaboration is not occurring and something must be done before further damage occurs.

How then can the facilitator intervene? The beauty of people is that they are always motivated by good intention. Even demonizing has a positive underpinning, and it is that positive *intention* that the facilitator can always help bring to light. For example:

Facilitator: Mrs. Jones, you seem to have some strong feelings right now. [transformative, reflecting for recognition]

Parent: I am not going to let that power-hungry egomaniac keep my child from the services he needs! [demonizing and accusing]

Facilitator: This is an important issue for you, and you must have good reasons for feeling this way. [facilitative, affirming the "important" and the "good"]

Parent: Well, yes it is! Johnny has been working really hard lately and showing lots of progress, and I think to move him out of a classroom where he has been doing so well just because he had one episode of temper—when he wasn't being properly supervised by that teacher—is not fair, and I'm not going to let them do that.

Facilitator: So if a child is making progress, he should be given every opportunity to continue on a successful path, is that it? [transformative, reframing for recognition]

Parent: Yes. Exactly. It's absurd to let one isolated incident ruin an otherwise good thing.

Facilitator: A child should be given more than just one chance, is that what you mean? [transformative, reframing]

Parent: Yes. [intensity is reduced, as usually happens when one has a chance to speak and be heard]

Facilitator: So where would you like to go with that? [transformative, empowerment]

Parent: What do you mean?

Facilitator: Well, you said that Johnny should be given another chance. So what would you like to do next? [recognition followed by empowerment]

Parent: I ought to call my lawyer and just get out of this stupid meeting.

Facilitator: Is that what you want to do now? [empowerment]

Parent: I want *him (sneers at administrator)* to keep my child in his classroom.

Facilitator: And so what do you want to do here—if you want Mr. Smith to keep Johnny in his present classroom? [empowerment and recognition]

Parent: *(turning to administrator)* Are you willing to keep Johnny where he is now?

Special education teacher: Could we ask the special education director to help us arrange for a behavioral intervention plan?

Administrator: How can we protect the other children from another outburst in the meantime?

Parent: What if you got him a one-to-one aide?

Special education teacher: I think a partition might be better for the short term.

And the team is once again collaborating—communicating well, exploring options, sharing ideas, remembering the child—and the facilitator can go back in the cuckoo clock.

Consider the alternatives. Without facilitation, an incident such as this one can easily become like a spark in a dry forest. A spark *by itself* may be small and easily managed, but it does not take long for it to lead to a fire raging out of control. This is what must not be allowed to occur, as so easily could without a facilitator:

Parent: *(pointing at administrator)* I am not going to let that power-hungry egomaniac keep my child from the services he needs!

Classroom teacher: But I can't have him kicking me and throwing tantrums in my class. I have 23 other children to take care of.

(Parent fumes.)

Administrator: I know how you feel, and I'm sorry you feel that way, Mrs. Jones. We all want to see your child succeed, but we have to look out for the others, too, as I'm sure you understand.

Parent: No, you *don't* know how I feel! You think you can just take the easy way out when children have special requirements that maybe don't fit with what you want from them. You have a legal responsibility to keep my child in a least restrictive environment—

Administrator: *(more forcefully)* Mrs. Jones, Mrs. Jones, please control yourself. Remember our ground rule about being respectful.

Parent: I will *not* control myself. I'm out of here. I can't believe you. You call yourselves educators and professionals. You're nothing but a bunch of hypocrites. It would be a whole different story if it were *your* child we were talking about. *(storms out and files a request for a due process hearing, alleging that her child is being denied his legal entitlement to a free and appropriate education in a least restrictive environment)*

Life is full of junctures just like this one, and the potential for escalation from sparks to flames is ever present when people have strong feelings and differing views. Yet given the right support, such sparks can be caught before any damage is done and can be redirected to promote deepening understanding and mutual agreement. It is the role of the facilitator to provide just such support.

Focusing on Competing Positions

Culturally speaking, very few of us have learned how to negotiate. It was probably not a course we took in school, and it is not necessarily modeled for us by peers or parents or depicted on television. It is not that we do not want to negotiate effectively; it is just that very few of us know how. And culturally speaking, the grave error we continually make is to lock into *positions*—forming a strong attachment to the things we say we want at the expense of a thorough understanding of why it is we want them. The thing we want, instead of the reason we want it, can also be called the *option* (instead of the interest), and yet it is the exploration of underlying *interests* that is the very key to building consensus, helping people to move from their strong feelings and differing perspectives into agreement.

The exploration of interests was popularized in a very well-known and highly recommended book called *Getting to Yes* (Fisher, Ury & Patton, 1992). It is also discussed in *A Guide to Collaboration for IEP Teams* (Martin, 2005). For now, it is enough to simply consider that team members tend to get themselves stuck in an entrenched focus on the things they say they want but have a very limited range of tools for making progress when they do not want the same *things*. This is what such entrenched positions can look like:

Parent: I want you to get my child a one-to-one aide in the classroom. He needs that kind of support and isn't ready to be independent.

Administrator: I hear what you're saying, Mrs. Green, but there are a lot of downsides to one-to-ones, and actually the district has very few available now, given the budget cuts we've recently had.

Parent: Well, you gave an aide to Melanie Gonzalez, so I know you can do it if you want to.

Administrator: I'm sorry, but I really can't talk about other children because of confidentiality.

Parent: Well, the point is that when *you* think a child needs one, she gets one, but if I think my child needs one, you're saying *no*. So what am I supposed to make of that?

Special education teacher: Mrs. Green, I think we all agree that children should get what they need. It's just that we don't really think an aide is what will be helpful to him.

Parent: It's the money isn't it? You won't admit it, but you just don't want to spend the money. You said yourself that the budget cuts—

Administrator: Mrs. Green, I think what Mrs. Brown is trying to say is that a teacher's aide may not be the best option.

Parent: So what are you suggesting, then? Just leave him to struggle in a classroom that is not providing for his needs?

Administrator: Well, maybe with a little more support in the home and—

Parent: Oh, are you saying it's my fault? You're saying support in the home but you won't give support in the school? Now I've heard it all!

A close look at this discussion reveals a focus on one thing (the aide), with people arguing about whether to provide that thing and getting increasingly upset and frustrated when others will not agree to provide the thing. In the parlance of negotiation, things are options, and by locking into a certain option, people take a position. Then, very often, when they do not get the thing they are asking for, they hire a lawyer or an advocate to help them get it; if this does not work, they look to the state department of education or to a court of law to ensure that they get it. Surely there's a better way! There *is*: leaving the options aside and instead focusing on the *interests*.

> Positions divide us; interests unite us.

The saying "Positions divide us, interests unite us" is deeply meaningful, and a simple illustration will help to clarify why. Let's explore Mrs. Green's strong attachment to the teacher's aide in the previous example. And let's imagine that instead of arguing with her, the team tries to understand her by asking interest-oriented questions. If the team members knew how to do this on their own, they probably would not need a facilitator. If, however, they do not know how to do this, then this is precisely the support the facilitator can bring. Let's pretend the team really does know, without a facilitator, how to leave options aside and explore their interests:

Parent: I want you to get my child a one-to-one aide in the classroom. He needs that kind of support and isn't ready to be independent.

Administrator: You must have good reasons for feeling this way, Mrs. Green. Can you help us understand what they are?

Parent: Well, if he had an aide, he would be more focused.

Administrator: And if he were more focused, what do you see happening then?

Parent: He would get better grades.

Administrator: And if he got better grades?

Parent: Well, if he got better grades, he would enjoy learning.

Special education teacher: What benefits could we expect if he enjoyed learning?

Parent: He would graduate.

Administrator: And after he graduates?

Parent: He would get a decent job and lead a normal life.

There is much to learn from this example, which is summarized in Table 3.1. Among the many insights are the following:

1.   The first answer a person gives may or may not be the heart of the matter— meaning the fundamental driving force behind the person's attachment to a particular option (i.e., their position).

2.   People *always* and only want something because of some anticipated future benefit, and that future benefit is their interest. The "so that . . . " is a connection between the thing and the anticipated outcome (e.g., so that he would be more focused, so that he would get better grades, so that he would enjoy learning).

Table 3.1   Exploring interests: Example

Progressive clarity (so that. . .)
Parent demands a teacher's aide so that the child may
• Stay more focused
• Get better grades
• Enjoy learning
• Graduate
• Get a good job
• Lead a normal life

3. If a parent believes that a teacher's aide is the best or perhaps the only way to ensure the successful life she desires for her child, she may be willing to go to very great lengths to fight for that good intention. This can explain some of the intensity that parents may bring to the IEP table, often to the surprise of school professionals.

4. Parents and school personnel may differ greatly in the positions that they take, and they may make very little progress if their focus remains at that level.

5. Although their positions may divide them, team members will usually be united in *all* of their interests. In the present example, everyone at the table wants the child to be more focused, get better grades, enjoy learning, graduate, get a good job, and prepare for a successful future.

Benefits of Exploring Interests

By considering the implications of this dichotomy of positions versus interests, it becomes obvious why the exploration of interests should be such an important part of the collaboration process. Exploring interests has several significant benefits:

1. **Raising self-awareness.** When people say they want something, they are not always aware of why it is they want it—that is, what their good intentions really are. Thus, the exploration of interests helps to bring these intentions into focus for the person himself or herself.

2. **Clarifying the interests for the group.** Now perhaps the whole group can see the good intention behind the demand and why this particular thing is so important to the person asking for it. The team will be more able to consider it, less likely to make assumptions or demonize, and more able to respond rather than react to the proposal of the team member.

3. **Showing that the person's interests are heard.** Even when others may not agree with what we are asking for, it can be very affirming and helpful for people just to know that their interests have been heard and understood.

4. **Showing that the interests are shared.** Positions divide us, but interests unite us; when opponents *recognize* this, that they share the same interests, they are much less likely to be seen as opponents! Instead, participants have the opportunity to see one another as members of one unified team, addressing their common challenges for the benefit of their common goal: serving the one, same child.

Again, if the team members already knew how to explore their interests, there would probably be no need for a facilitator. It is a fairly safe assumption, then, that when a facilitator has been requested, the team will require assistance in this area. The facilitator can provide the needed support by watching for intervention points when the team members are locked into positions and frustrated that others are not responding as they would like them to. Helpful interventions will often include such statements as "You seem to have strong feelings . . . " "This seems to be an important issue . . . " "There seems to be something you want the team to recognize . . . " All of these are reflections for recognition, which are just one of a long list of intervention options which will be covered in the chapters ahead, especially Chapter 5.

Discounting the Team and Its Members

Discounting the team and its members is, of course, the opposite of valuing the team and its members. Indications that someone is being discounted include unkind remarks and accusations, hostility, anger, and similar signs that positive feelings have been replaced by negative ones and that effective communication has broken down. Because the remedies for this are so similar to those required for positive communication and for addressing unproductive communication styles, they are presented in those upcoming sections. For now, let it just be said that the facilitator must be ever on the alert for when team members are discounting one another and thus heading down a path that is sure to keep them from collaborating and reaching their goals.

Losing Faith in the Process

Even at their angriest and even in their darkest moments, it is possible that team members retain *some* faith in their process. If not, one or more members would probably be seeing the discussions as hopeless and suggesting that the meeting be terminated. Some of the tools the facilitator can use to buoy the team members' confidence include reflecting the agreements they have made and, especially, opening new lines of communication when the team appears to be stuck. Because dealing with impasse is the subject of Chapter 6, just one example is presented here of a scenario in which a facilitator might intervene to restore trust in the collaborative process. There are two key elements in this example: 1) the parent has given up, and 2) the team does not know how to move forward.

Parent: This is a waste of time. You all are going to do what you plan to do anyway, so I don't see any point in continuing this meeting.

Teacher: Mr. Chen, you just need to see how much Erica is progressing without additional services.

Parent: I'm just not going to continue this discussion. She needs additional tutoring in reading or she'll just fall further behind. It's your job to provide it. I don't see why this is too much to ask!

Administrator: We can't just provide additional tutoring for every child in the school, Mr. Chen. We have to base our interventions on identified needs, and I just don't think Erica needs more services. She needs to take better advantage of the services that she already has. That's why we suggest a behavior incentive program.

(Parent fumes and sulks, might easily storm out, and has clearly lost faith in the process; the facilitator now intervenes.)

Facilitator: Team, it seems like you've hit a rough spot here. [reflecting for recognition]

Parent: There's no point continuing a discussion where no one's willing to hear anything that doesn't fit with what they came here already thinking.

Facilitator: So you're saying there's a different way the team could be communicating today? [beginning to reframe for recognition]

Parent: Yes!

Facilitator: What might that be?

Parent: Well, I think it has to start with more open minds.

Facilitator: So, open minds would be helpful. [reframing for recognition; who can argue with this general principle?]

Parent: Yes.

(Eerie silence; facilitator allows the tension to just be for a moment.)

Teacher: What if we reassess the tutoring plan Erica has right now and maybe set some more specific goals that can be monitored in the short term? Rather than add tutoring, we could maybe redesign the tutoring she has now.

Parent: How long are we going to wait to watch her fail?

Facilitator: This is an important issue for you—that she makes progress and maintains gains, right? [reflecting for recognition and reframing; note that the teacher has made a new proposal but not one that clearly addresses the parent's interest that the child not fall further behind; note also that the facilitator has reframed the parent's statement in terms of what he *does* want rather than what he does not]

Parent: Yes, exactly. We need to intervene right now and not wait!

Facilitator: So what if you were to maybe try a redesigned program for, say, 2 or 3 weeks, and, if she shows no signs of progress, then get right back together and reassess? Would that be an idea of any value? What do you all think? [facilitative model, playing with the "time shape" of a proposal, something the team may not have thought of as an option]

Administrator: I'm not sure signs of progress can be expected in only 2 or 3 weeks.

Reading specialist: Well, I think it depends on how we establish the goals, but I think we could know by then whether we are on the right track or not.

Facilitator: So how does that sound to everyone—workable, reasonable, or maybe not?

(The team members nod in consensus; a bridge over their divisions has been built and collaboration has been restored.)

PROMOTING POSITIVE COMMUNICATION

Some of what relates to promoting positive communication has already been illustrated in several hypothetical scenarios. In some ways, supporting positive communication is what facilitation is really *all* about, because true collaboration and positive communication are integrally connected; you can't have one without the other. Rather than try and cover this very broad subject here and now, let's just focus on one essential intervention skill that greatly supports positive communication: reframing.

Reframes

The word *reframe* will probably not appear in most dictionaries, yet it is a well-known term among counselors, mediators, and similar professionals who study the details of interpersonal interactions and how to support people to communicate more productively. *Reframing* can be defined in part as restating a communication so as to make it more positive. Thus, "He's a real jerk" might be restated as "You take issue with some things he does." "She never cares about anyone but herself" might be restated as "You would like her to be more open to your thoughts and feelings." In terms of facilitation, however, this process of taking a negative and phrasing it more positively is only half the task of reframing. The other half is to take it out of polarity and into unity. This, of course, warrants explanation.

The fundamental premise or vision of collaboration is of one team working together in unity, synergy, and togetherness, in contrast to a team divided by adversity, opposition, conflict, and sides. Whenever a negative is phrased in terms of "you feel he . . . " or "you think she . . . ," separation and adversity are underscored. The challenge for the ideal reframe is to phrase the statement not just more positively but in terms that *all* can espouse. Thus, "He's a real jerk" might be reframed as "We should be open minded and work together for the benefit of the child" (who can argue with that?), and "She never cares about anyone but herself" might be rephrased as "It's important that all views be considered" (again, something all will accept). In both examples, the point is to replace the "you/me" or "us/them" with a statement that both reflects the good intention of the communicator *and* puts it in a form that all can accept.

Let's back up and consider why reframing is such an important tool in the facilitator's skill set. Whenever people are in conflict and have bad feelings, there will be a tendency to demonize—to see the other person in globally negative terms. This is to be expected, and thus during contentious meetings, some of this demonizing, anger, and hostility is almost sure to surface. Unless the facilitator can capture the negativity and redirect it, it will be like a torpedo that *will* find its mark and will be destructive. Furthermore, the negative digs that team members often make toward one another are cumulative. They fester, they grow, they build on one another, and they lead to nothing but harm. However, the negativity that any member brings to the table has at least two very *positive* sides. First, because people are always well intentioned, whatever it is they are saying will invariably reflect something good! Second, verbalizing the negatives offers an opportunity for healing and restoration, and, if managed effectively, it can help transform the old and unproductive into the new and more productive. This growth and healing is the opportunity and potential offered by the facilitation process, hence the term *transformative* facilitation—transforming relationships.

The Simple Rule of Reframing

From negative to positive
From polarity to unity

Reframing involves being able to consider what a person does not want (e.g., for her to not care about anyone but herself) and then look to what he or she *does* want (e.g., for her to care about others). Thus, "You want her to be open to the feelings and opinions of others" takes this comment from the negative to the positive, and then "The team should be open to the thoughts of all of its members" takes that good intention and phrases it in unity. Isn't this a value everyone is likely to accept? Is anyone at the IEP meeting likely to think, "No, we should be completely closed to other people's opinions"?

It is usually best to end reframes with a question in order to leave the door open for any clarification or correction that may be necessary. In addition to "capturing the torpedoes" before they do damage, reframes serve to promote awareness, which is recognition. If the facilitator's reframe is not very accurate, then the speaker can help to clarify more precisely what was meant. The process is still a good one, and the facilitator can beam with pride at being wrong. For example:

Parent: (to teacher) You are so closed minded—you're not even listening.

Facilitator: So are you saying that the team should be open to the views of all of its members? [reframe]

Parent: No. I'm saying that this proposal has some benefits that she's not willing to see.

Facilitator: So when a suggestion is made, it is important for the team to understand the reasons behind it and the benefits it may offer? [more accurate reframe]

Parent: Yes.

In this example, the facilitator's initial reframe was not quite what the speaker meant to say. Well, fine! The facilitator can rejoice that he was wrong because the process has worked to a successful conclusion; the more accurate positive message has been clarified and recognition has now occurred.

Two-Stage Reframes

Should the facilitator always be able to determine what the speaker intends? Is this a reasonable expectation? What if he or she has no clue at all? An easy solution is the *two-stage reframe:* The facilitator can simply begin by assuming the speaker is seeing a better way, or a different way, or another way. The speaker is sure to say yes, or he or she would not have had his or her feathers so ruffled. The next question then is "What might that be?" or "What might that look like?" The whole process looks like this:

Administrator: (to parent) You're just not getting it.

Facilitator: Are you saying there's a different way the team could be communicating?

Administrator: Well, yes.

Facilitator: And what might that look like?

Administrator: Well, I think, if she would just consider other people's views and not be so locked into her own way of seeing things, we might make some progress here.

Facilitator: Are you saying that team members need to be willing to consider the merits of all of the views being shared? Is that it?

Administrator: Yes.

Again, the administrator might have said no and then offered greater clarification of what he was trying to say, but let's assume that the final reframe was correct. What happened is that the facilitator, sensing the administrator's frustration, began by asking about a different way, which the administrator then clarified. The administrator's communication was still couched in negativity and polarity, which the facilitator was then able to restate from negative to positive and from polarity to unity.

Once again, two-stage reframes usually involve a first question about a different, a better, or another way and then a second question along the lines of "What would that look like?" that brings into focus what the speaker thinks that better way might be. Once clarified, the facilitator can then hold it up for all to see in the form of a one-stage reframe, as presented earlier: "So the team should . . . , is that it?"

Here are a few exercises in reframing. See if you can guess the good intention of the speaker. Then take the comment from negative to positive and from polarity to unity; that is, from what the speaker does not want to what he or she does want, and from what the speaker alone wants to what the group as a whole might want. Model responses appear in Appendix D.

Exercises in Reframing

Imagine a participant at an IEP meeting makes the following remarks to another participant. How could the statements be reframed to make them positive ones that all members would accept?

Example: She only feels bad because she thinks we don't care.

Reframe: It's important that you all can trust each other's motivations, is that it?

1. You're being totally unreasonable and not listening to anything we say.

2. You're always so negative; you need to think more positively.

3. You should at least want to understand before being so quick to argue.

4. You're interrupting me and raising your voice again.

5. Why do you always think someone's out to get you?

6. Can't you just wait a minute and let me finish what I'm trying to say?

7. I don't think she can follow all that school jargon.

8. Would you have the courtesy to at least not shout and call names?

9. Maybe if you would spend more time with your child, he would do better.

10. I'm really getting tired of your threatening to get a lawyer.

Helping to Explore Interests

Earlier in this chapter, the exploration of underlying interests was discussed and some references were provided for further study (see "Focusing on Competing Positions"). Rather than repeat that information, here is a list of questions that help clarify the interests of a person who is making a demand.

Questions that Probe for Underlying Interests

You must have good reasons for thinking this; can you tell us some of them?

Where do you think that would lead?

Can you say some more about that; how might that address the issue?

What would it look like if the team were to do that?

What do you see happening if you all go that route?

How might that idea be helpful?

What benefits could be expected if you did that?

HELPING ENSURE THAT EVERYONE IS "ON THE SAME PAGE"

One of the tasks of the facilitator is to be alert to whether the team is "on the same page." This is an interesting idiom and a deeply meaningful one. If the team is *not* on the same page, then what might that look like? Perhaps team members are focused on different topics, are distracted by bad feelings or confusion, or simply do not understand the terminology or the task at hand. In any of these instances, collaboration has broken down—the team is not working together toward common objectives. These then become critical points for intervention, and recognition and empowerment are probably all that will be necessary. Here is an example:

Teacher: I think the real issue is how to hold his attention. He is so easily distracted, especially if he is not directly engaged at that moment.

Parent: He has no trouble focusing when he is watching *Barney.* There's something about that show that really speaks to him. I haven't seen anything like it.

Teacher: Well, the issue is what we can do in the classroom. I think some supports are necessary just to help keep him on task. Otherwise, he becomes restless and starts showing behaviors that disrupt the other children.

Parent: This doesn't happen at home, because for one thing there aren't other children around him.

Teacher: But, Mrs. Flores, I can't be giving him undivided attention all the time. I do have to attend to the other children.

Parent: *(mutters)* But he has a right to be in your classroom. *(becomes silent)*

Facilitator: *(sees that the teacher and parent are not on the same page: the parent is focused on the difference between classroom and home behaviors, and the teacher is focused on the challenge of preventing disruption while helping the child stay on task)* So may I just see if I understand what you're saying. Mrs. Flores? You see that Andrew has a great potential to stay on task, right? [repeating for recognition]

Parent: Yes. At home he can be very focused. That's what I'm trying to say. He just needs something that interests him and a certain amount of personalized attention.

Facilitator: *(to teacher)* And you're saying that his behavior can make it hard for you to attend to the other children, is that it? [repeating for recognition]

Teacher: Yes, exactly. He needs a lot more support than I can give him.

Facilitator: So he needs more support, but with the right supports, he can stay focused, right? [repeating for recognition] *(Parent nods, teacher looks unsure)* So where would you like to go with that? [empowerment]

Teacher: *(to team)* I don't know. Anyone have any suggestions?

Special education teacher: I think we could maybe try a buddy system for him. If another child could work with him, then the burden could be taken off the teacher and it might work.

Director of special education: This has certainly worked with other children. I think it's worth a try.

The group is collaborating again; they are back on the same page of exploring a common challenge and working together to develop an IEP that will meet the needs of that particular child.

CLARIFYING AREAS OF AGREEMENT

Why should a facilitator clarify areas of agreement? After all, if the team is making agreements, isn't that proof positive that the members are collaborating successfully and that the facilitator therefore has no role to play? Well, the answer is yes and no. The real issue is whether the team *recognizes* that it has made agreements. There are at least three specific scenarios in which some support may be warranted.

Clarifying for Recognition

The first scenario in which support may be warranted is when the team members *seem* to have made agreements but the agreements are not clear and the members may not recognize that an agreement has been made. Rather than let this ball get dropped, the facilitator can help clarify the agreement for purposes of recognition. For example:

Teacher: Well, I think career counseling during the zero hour at the start of the day would be a good time, because then she wouldn't miss any classes.

Parent: I wonder if she would enjoy hairstyling as a profession. She spends a lot of time doing her makeup and things, and she has even cut her sister's bangs, and she did it very well.

Administrator: I think that is a very real possibility, and it would be great to see her finding something that sparks her passion. So are we ready to talk about any changes we might want to make to the IEP?

(Team members nod in agreement.)

Facilitator: *(sees that the group is moving on and yet an implied agreement has not been made clear)* May I just ask a question? You seemed to agree that zero hour would be the best time for her career counseling, is that right?

Teacher: *(to parent)* I think that would be best, don't you?

Parent: Yes, I think that would be fine.

In this scenario, the implied agreement was clarified for all to see and to invite any necessary correction if in fact agreement had *not* been reached. Consider the implications of not providing this support for recognition. There is a possibility that an agreement was *not* actually made and that the members will leave the meeting with different expectations, which might later lead to disappointment, irritation, and a failure to fulfill an agreement that was *assumed* to have been made. Imagine, for example, that the parent later finds out that the student attended career counseling during history class; she might then become annoyed that the staff had not fulfilled what she had understood to be an agreement to arrange the counseling during the time when her daughter had no classes at the start of the day.

Restoring Faith in the Process

A second scenario in which clarifying points of agreement might be helpful is when the team members have lost sight of their progress and have perhaps lost hope as well, seeing only the negative. Recall that one of the seven keys to collaboration is trusting the collaborative process. If this trust is lost, the potential for success may be lost alongside it. For example:

Parent: If you're not going to get the one-to-one aide, then it's a waste of time to continue this meeting. I'm out of here.

Advocate: *(to parent)* I think it's obvious you're going to have to take this to a higher level.

Administrator: Mr. Washington, as much as I'd like to give you what you are asking for, I just don't feel that it's in your child's best interests.

Parent: I'm out of here.

Facilitator: *(sees that the team members have lost faith in their process and are focused only on their one point of disagreement after many points of agreement)* I sense some frustrations in the room. Would it make sense to maybe summarize what seems to have happened during this meeting? I've noticed a lot of progress made and quite a few points of agreement. [reflecting for recognition and asking permission to repeat for recognition]

Parent: Well, I don't see it, but go ahead.

(Other members nod in agreement.)

Facilitator: Well, please correct me if I'm wrong here. I think you all agreed that eligibility is still appropriate, right? And it sounds like everyone is seeing considerable progress in reading, am I right? And I noticed that you seemed in agreement that some follow-up testing would be a good thing prior to the next state testing, no? And I think you agreed that math continues to be very challenging for Mary and that additional help of some sort is going to be important. And you all seemed to share a concern with the question of timely exchange of information and proposed a plan whereby the teacher will call home and not just rely on Mary to share the message if it is something really important for the parents to receive. Am I right so far? *(Group nods in approval.)* Wow, sounds like you agreed on quite a lot today. So, then, the only point that seems really undecided is whether a teacher's aide is going to be the best way to give Mary the support in math class that you all agree is necessary. Am I wrong about that?

Parent: Well, she needs support, and I don't see why having an adult to work closely with her wouldn't be a simple solution to this problem. I think it's just the money. They don't want to spend the money.

Administrator: I'm not going to lie and say that the money isn't something we want to consider. I just assure you that it is not the deciding factor. I wouldn't recommend a teacher's aide for math support even if we had all the money in the world. It would just make her very dependent, and this could be very harmful for her in the long run.

Teacher: So what do you propose?

Administrator: Well, I'm not sure yet. How about we ask for a recommendation from the Education Service Center and meet again in, say, 2 weeks, to continue this discussion?

Parent: Okay, but I'm not sure I believe you.

Facilitator: So it sounds like you are agreed to have an expert make suggestions about how best to support Mary's math skills and then to meet again in 2 weeks to consider her recommendations, is that right?

(All nod in agreement.)

In this example, the process of reflecting the many agreements made while clarifying the one point of disagreement helped to restore faith in the process and assisted the team to continue collaborating. Without such support, the parent might easily have left the meeting in disgust, and a complaint investigation or due process hearing might have been an unnecessary next step.

Clarifying Shared Interests and Shared Risks

There is a third scenario in which clarifying areas of agreement may help preserve collaboration toward consensus. At every IEP meeting, all members have certain shared interests and shared risks (see Table 3.2). Avoiding a shared risk is always a shared interest. Yet how can a facilitator use this very important general principle? The following example builds on the previous scenario but assumes that the parent remains firm in his desire to end the meeting and take the matter to a higher authority:

Parent: If you're not going to get the one-to-one aide, then it's a waste of time to continue this meeting. I'm out of here.

Advocate: *(to parent)* I think it's obvious you're going to have to take this to a higher level.

Table 3.2. Shared interests and shared risks: Avoiding a shared risk is always a shared interest.

Shared interests	Shared risks
To serve the best interests of the child	Wasted time
To be heard	Damaged future relationships
To be understood	Escalating tensions
To be respected	Due process hearings
To have a voice	
To make good use of time	
To be treated fairly	
To be productive	
To feel safe and comfortable	

Administrator: Mr. Washington, as much as I'd like to give you what you are asking for, I just don't feel that it's in your child's best interests.

Parent: I'm out of here.

Facilitator: *(sees that the meeting is about to end with failure to reach agreement and a loss of collaboration)* Mr. Washington, I hear you saying that this is a waste of time and you're out of here, is that right? [repeating for recognition]

Parent: Right.

Facilitator: *(shifts from the transformative to the facilitative approach because it seems clear that the team is unlikely to resolve this on its own)* Is everyone in agreement that terminating the meeting now would be your best next step? Does anyone see any downsides to leaving at this point? [probing for interests— what they see as their shared risks]

Administrator: Well, I think we could work this out if Mr. Washington would just work with us.

Facilitator: So you think there is still hope to work this out? [repeating for recognition]

Administrator: Yes, I do.

Facilitator: *(seeing that the question of downsides was not answered)* Does anyone see any downsides if you did just end the meeting at this point? [probing for interests]

Special education teacher: Well, I think Mr. Washington is talking about a due process hearing or complaint with the state, and I think that would be very unfortunate.

Facilitator: Very unfortunate. [repeating for recognition]

Special education teacher: Well, yes. It would take so much time and lead to so much bad feeling. It's just not necessary.

Facilitator: So you see some downsides in the time involved and the damage to your team relationships, is that right? *(Special education teacher nods in agreement.)* So does everyone agree that this might lead to lots of time spent and lots of bad feelings? *(All agree; parent seems to be stopping to consider.)* I suspect nobody wants to see your relationships damaged or time wasted if it isn't necessary, am I right? [reflecting the team's common interest in avoiding two shared risks] *(All nod in agreement.)* So does anyone see any options? [asking for help]

Administrator: *(to parent)* Mr. Washington, I hope you will continue to explore options with us and see if we can't work this out.

Teacher: I'd like you to give us a chance.

Advocate: *(to parent)* You can always file later if you want to.

Parent: Okay. So what else could you do for my daughter, if you won't get her an aide?

And the team is collaborating once again.

One final note about clarifying areas of agreement. It might seem that the facilitator in the previous scenario has stepped across the line and become attached to an agreement—to settlement. After all, there was a parenthetical comment early in the example that the facilitator "sees that the meeting is about to end with failure to reach agreement." This issue warrants clarification.

The goals of the transformative and facilitative styles are to promote recognition and empowerment (transformative) or productive dialogue (facilitative). In both models, whether a settlement is reached is entirely up to the parties. In the preceding scenario, the facilitator's intention is not to ensure settlement but rather to give the parties every opportunity to recognize their lost hope, to recognize their shared interests and shared risks, and to then be empowered to make a free but informed decision. The question of settlement remains entirely up to them.

ADDRESSING UNPRODUCTIVE COMMUNICATION STYLES

Because effective communication is so essential to collaboration, the ability to address unproductive communication styles is an essential skill in the facilitator's toolbox. There are many forms of unproductive communication. Perhaps the most obvious are shouting, name calling, and similar hostility, yet there are others, such as withdrawal, interrupting, side talking, and rambling. What they have in common is that they all obstruct collaboration and undermine the probability of the team achieving its goal of effectively planning for the education of the child.

There are many intervention options available to the skilled facilitator, and these will be covered in Chapter 5. For now, we can simply reference several that have already been presented: reflecting, repeating, or reframing for recognition; empowering; asking about ground rules; pausing for reflection; and asking for help. Many examples of addressing unproductive communication styles have already been presented; others appear in the chapters ahead.

HELPING TO BRING MEANINGFUL CLOSURE

Assisting with bringing meaningful closure is the last on the list of roles of the skilled facilitator. Just as the opening remarks at the beginning of the meeting are the responsibility of the chairperson, so also is ending the meeting in an appropriate way. But does the chairperson know how to do this? Possibly not, and for this reason the facilitator should be prepared to assist.

Let's begin by asking what "meaningful closure" really means. Why not simply say "bye-bye" at the end of the meeting and leave it at that? What might be the drawbacks to ending the meeting with a simple good-bye? Well, some members of the team may have additional comments or questions that perhaps they have not yet had a chance to voice. People might leave with a lack of clarity about what has been agreed and what their next steps should be. There would be a lost opportunity for a short debriefing to discuss how the meeting went and how the next meeting might be even better as a result. Finally, ending with a simple good-bye misses the opportunity to end on a positive note—to thank all of the participants for their time and contributions and thank the team for allowing the facilitator to be a part of the meeting.

Promoting Meaningful Closure

1. Address questions or concerns
2. Clarify next steps
3. Get feedback for the future
4. End on a positive note

The chairperson will probably cover at least some of these elements as the participants prepare to leave the meeting. If not, here are some things the facilitator might say, and the word *might* is appropriate here. There is nothing absolute about these points, and yet they may be helpful if, in the facilitator's judgment, they "fit with the flow":

1. "Before we leave, may I just ask if everyone has had a chance to raise any questions or share any thoughts that perhaps they didn't yet have a chance to do?"

2. "Is everyone clear on the plan from this point forward—your next steps and who will be taking them? Would it be of any value to summarize the main points of your agreement today?"

3. "How are you all feeling about your meeting today—anything you might want to be sure to do again next time, or maybe anything you would want to do differently next time?"

4. "I want to thank you all for doing such a great job of collaborating today and for giving me this opportunity to work with you."

4 | Planning and Guiding the Meeting

In this chapter, we will revisit several topics mentioned in Chapter 3 in the discussion of the roles of the facilitator, examining them in greater detail along with different sample scenarios. The topics are also presented here for purposes of organization, to serve as a handy reference for the facilitator who must ensure that these issues are properly addressed. Toward the end of this chapter, I will discuss the special challenges presented when attorneys or advocates are attending the meeting.

BEFORE THE MEETING

The first thing the facilitator must be sure to do before the IEP meeting is to contact both the chairperson and the parent.

Contacting the Chairperson

When contacting the chairperson, the facilitator should

1. Explain his or her role as to support the team members to communicate well and to achieve their objectives for the child

2. Explain that he or she is not a decision maker, is not there to give advice or share expertise, and may actually spend a lot of time just quietly listening

3. Encourage the chairperson to have a written agenda, to set guidelines (ground rules), to begin with introductions, to ask about projected time frames in case anyone must leave early, and to have tissues and refreshments on the table. A sample IEP meeting agenda might be shared with the chairperson prior to the meeting, and one is provided in Appendix C.

4. Ask that the chairperson read and circulate an "agreement to facilitation" for all participants to sign at the start of the meeting. A sample agreement form is provided in Appendix K.

5. Encourage the chairperson to notify the other committee members that the facilitator will be attending so that all members know in advance what to expect

6. Invite the chairperson to ask any questions

It is very common for the chairperson (and the parent) to want to tell the facilitator the history that has led to the request for facilitation. This might begin with such questions as "Should I tell you what has been happening in this case?" or "Should I give you a little insight into the history we have had with this parent?" The challenge for the facilitator is to be respectful and to show genuine interest and yet not to spend a lot of time in discussions that have absolutely no bearing on what will happen during the facilitation, while also minimizing the probability of negative expectations on the facilitator's part.

Let's look more closely at this issue of the facilitator's expectations. As mentioned in Chapter 3, the tendency to demonize is to be expected when people are in an unresolved conflict. The chairperson is thus likely to portray the parent as unreasonable, belligerent, unaware, or demanding. And the parent is likely to do exactly the same thing, describing the school personnel as just trying to get by with the minimal amount of work necessary, not really caring about the child, only concerned about money, closed to any opinions but their own, and so forth. The facilitator needs to be alert not to buy into these globally negative perceptions but instead to see them as just a manifestation of the conflict he or she has been asked to help resolve. Incidentally, this is not to suggest that every facilitated IEP meeting has a history of unresolved conflict or that whenever a facilitator has been requested it can be assumed that the team members are in serious dispute. A facilitator might be requested to assist a team that has actually been collaborating well, and yet this is probably the exception rather than the rule. But, if there *has* been a history of conflict and if negative perceptions do surface, it is recommended that the facilitator think positively—only positively—and assume good reason and intention, as mentioned in Chapter 3. Not only do people generally have good reasons and good intentions, there is also the issue of the self-fulfilling prophecy.

A *self-fulfilling prophecy* is a process by which expectations tend to fulfill themselves—that what people expect, they tend to attract, create, or promote. Then when things happen as they expected, they say, "I told you so," and the expectation is strengthened. Thus, people who expect rejection and failure will tend to encounter rejection and failure, whereas those who expect acceptance and success will tend to encounter acceptance and success. In the facilitation arena, having the expectation that people have good reasons and are well intentioned tends to promote the experience of that very thing. Believing leads to seeing.

A few words are also in order concerning the issue of not spending time in discussions that will have no bearing on what will happen during the meeting. One might assume that the facilitator will be all the more prepared if he or she has a thorough understanding of all that has happened that has led the team to request outside help. But why? How does this knowledge help the facilitator in any way? After all, his or her role is not to resolve anything, not to answer any questions, not to advise on courses of action, but instead only to support the team members to do the one and only thing they may have been unable to do on their own: reach consensus through collaboration. Had they been able to do that, or had they felt confident that they *could* do that, they would probably not be asking for facilitation. The facilitator must remain very clear about his or her role being *only* to support the team's collaborative process. For this reason, the *less* the facilitator knows about the case, the better!

The question then becomes, how can the facilitator show interest and respect when it is obvious that the chairperson or the parent wants to tell the whole story in perhaps infinite detail? Perhaps the best way is to be prepared to explain the following:

1. **I intend to be an unbiased, third party.** I plan to be impartial to any particular side, person, or position. At the same time, I want to be respectful and supportive of all of the team members' thoughts and opinions. I would ask that any member be willing to let me know if at any time I do not appear to be interested or respectful or impartial.

2. **I know very little about the team's past experience,** but I see that as a good thing—it can help me be open to learning about you as a team and what you all think is best as you develop the student's IEP.

3. **As a facilitator, I am here as an assistant,** not an advisor, not a decision maker, and not an expert. In fact, mine is the only opinion here that really doesn't matter. I'm just here to help you work together more effectively for the benefit of the student and make decisions you can all feel good about.

4. **My role is to assist you in achieving your objectives** and to support you in sharing what you bring as a valued member of the team.

More specifically, if the chairperson should ask, "May I tell you what has happened in this case?" the facilitator might respond by saying, for example, "If you want to tell me anything at all, I am certainly interested. At the same time, I generally consider it an advantage not to know a lot about what has happened so that I can come in with an open mind and be focused more on the collaborative process for you all as a team." If the chairperson continues to offer details, the facilitator should then listen attentively and show support. The facilitator also can encourage the chairperson to share his or her concerns during the meeting, if the chairperson should want to do so. For example:

Chairperson: Well, I think she is just so locked into her insistence that we provide additional speech services, and she just isn't aware of what all we have to juggle to be able to do that. And her child doesn't really need them.

Facilitator: Sounds like there are a number of issues here that you would like her to see more clearly.

Chairperson: Well, exactly. She's just unwilling to see any view-points but her own.

Facilitator: So if she could see it from your point of view, it might open some new doors, is that what you're saying?

Chairperson: Definitely.

Facilitator: Is this something you might want to bring up at the meeting—that open minds and seeing all viewpoints could maybe help the team move forward?

Chairperson: Not that it would do any good.

Facilitator: Well, maybe this is an area where I could support you.

Chairperson: I'm willing to give it a try.

Contacting the Parent

The preconference with the parent will be similar but not quite the same as the preconference with the chairperson. The facilitator should

1. Explain his or her role as to support the team members to communicate well and to achieve their objectives for the child

2. Explain that he or she is not a decision maker, is not there to give advice or share expertise, and may actually spend a lot of time just quietly listening

3. Explain that he or she plans to be impartial and unbiased and to help the team work together effectively for the benefit of the child

4. Encourage the parent to inform whomever he or she may be bringing to the meeting in which the facilitator will be present

5. Invite the parent to ask any questions

With regard to informing others who will be attending the meeting, the parent may be bringing a spouse, an advocate, an ally, or an attorney. It is important that this support person also know that the facilitator will be present, so that he or she will not be unpleasantly surprised and will also know in advance what the facilitator's role will be. At times it might be helpful to offer to speak directly with that other person, especially if the parent thinks this would be helpful (e.g., as with an advocate or attorney). Who should call whom? The facilitator would typically initiate contact with the parent(s) but in most cases would then welcome any others to contact him or her, rather than the other way around.

An independent conversation initiated by the facilitator *would* be appropriate if an ex-spouse will also be attending the meeting. The facilitator should not just assume that if one spouse has agreed to facilitation, then the ex-spouse's opinion will either be the same or does not really matter. It does! What if an ex-spouse objects to a facilitator being present? There is probably a clear statement in the school files as to who has the authority to make such a decision. If an ex-spouse has the same legal authority as the spouse who has consented to facilitation and if, after a reasonable effort to explain the benefits of facilitation, the ex still refuses to agree to it, then the facilitator might have to respect the objection and not attend the meeting.

If the parent or his or her support person wishes to tell the facilitator the history of the case, the facilitator's response might be very similar to what was outlined in the scenario with the chairperson. The facilitator can be most helpful by always thinking positively, clarifying what the person wants (rather than what he or she does not want), and encouraging him or her to raise these same concerns at the meeting, assuring that the facilitator will be there to lend full support (to the process, not the content).

ARRIVING AT THE MEETING

On arriving at the meeting, the facilitator will want to bring hopefulness, friendliness, sincere smiles, and warm handshakes. His or her positive presence will have a beneficial influence on others, who have quite possibly arrived with apprehensions, doubts, and bad feelings from the past. A wonderful saying to consider is "What you are speaks so loudly I can't hear what you're saying." The facilitator can thus bring a great deal to the meeting just through his or her unspoken qualities and demeanor.

SETTING THE STAGE

Several elements *must* be in place to ensure the smooth running of the meeting. These include participant introductions, a written agenda, ground rules, projected time frames, and ideally some drinks and simple refreshments (e.g., bottled juices or water, cookies, crackers, candies). Because these will have been discussed in the preconference with the chairperson, the facilitator will not have to lead so much as gently remind the chairperson if any of these have been overlooked—and they *may* be overlooked because of lack of practice, distractions, or simply forgetfulness. Although refreshments are not a critical element, the others are, and those balls must not get dropped.

What follows is some sample wording that a facilitator might use if the relevant topics have not been addressed by the chairperson. But give him or her a reasonable chance—it may be that these items will be covered in a slightly different order or at a different time.

Introductions. Hi, my name is Richard Markham, and I'm [role: assistant principal over at Meadowlark Elementary; professor at Wooster University; volunteer facilitator from such-and-such an agency]. Ms. Kromer asked if I could attend this meeting to help you all come up with a great IEP for Holly. I haven't had the pleasure of meeting all of you yet. Could we maybe take a moment for each of us to say who we are and how we work with Holly? Would that be okay with you?

Agenda. I believe that today you will be doing an [nature of meeting, such as an annual or initial] IEP meeting. Would it be helpful to maybe jot down some of the key topics on the flip chart so you all will be able to see where you are and be sure all of the things get addressed? [allow response] Would anyone be willing to help with writing it? [allow response and then, once the topics have been made clear, ask] Does this seem like a reasonable plan for today?

Time projections. Could we take just a minute to talk about the structure of the meeting? Of course, we probably don't know exactly how long this meeting will take, but what would be a reasonable expectation? [allow response] It's now 1 p.m. Is everyone free to remain until, say, 3 p.m. if necessary? Would anyone have to leave before then?

Ground rules. Some teams find it helpful to have some guidelines for their meetings. These are sort of like proposals for what would help the meeting run more smoothly—like no interrupting and turning off cell phones. Is that something any of you would like to include today?

Snack items. I see some snack items and drinks here on the table—is everyone welcome to just dig in?

Again, all of these elements will have been discussed with the chairperson prior to the meeting. It is therefore usually unnecessary to do more than simply raise the issue and thereby provide just a friendly reminder. The same applies to the agreement to facilitation form; if the chairperson forgets, the facilitator can simply ask, "Were you going to discuss the agreement form?"

HANDLING OBJECTIONS

What if, perish the thought, the facilitator should introduce himself or herself and a member of the team objects, perhaps angrily, "Nobody told *me* you were coming!" Hopefully this will have been avoided entirely by preconferencing with the chairperson and the parent, and yet a skilled facilitator has to be prepared to address such a concern should it arise. Let's first consider some don'ts.

The tendency of the beginning facilitator might be to justify and defend his or her presence by giving an explanation, as in the following example:

Advocate: Nobody told *me* you were coming!

Facilitator: But I spoke with Mrs. Marek, and she assured me she would tell you.

What are the implications of such a response? In effect, it puts Mrs. Marek in the awkward position of having to confess to an error on her part (maybe she forgot to tell her advocate the facilitator would be coming). Or perhaps she did not forget and the advocate simply misunderstood; perhaps Mrs. Marek told the advocate that there would be facilitation, and the advocate assumed this just meant that the chairperson would be managing the meeting more effectively than before. Another possibility is that Mrs. Marek did explain it very clearly and the advocate simply forgot. In any event, the facilitator's response in this example is likely to put somebody in an awkward position and is thus unlikely to promote good feelings and a positive start to the meeting.

The following example illustrates another response to avoid:

Advocate: Nobody told *me* you were coming!

Facilitator: So you have some concerns about my being here?

Advocate: Well, actually, I do.

Facilitator: *(to team)* How do the rest of you feel?

By responding this way, the facilitator has polarized the group into those in favor versus those opposed to the facilitator's presence. It is very unlikely that the rest of the group members will agree that they have concerns, and so the scene may quickly develop into us against them, or school against parent and advocate. This may force the advocate to back down, walk out, or perhaps just silently fume at having been outvoted by the majority. Surely there are better ways for the facilitator to respond.

A final pitfall to avoid is the inclination to "lock horns" and try to persuade the person who is objecting to the facilitator's attendance:

Advocate: Nobody told *me* you were coming!

Facilitator: So you have some concerns about my being here?

Advocate: Well, actually, I do.

Facilitator: Well, my role is just to assist you all. I am not here to make decisions or give advice or take sides.

Advocate: But who asked you to be here?

Facilitator: I was invited by the chairperson, and I spoke to the parent, who also agreed.

Advocate: I just don't think that if you work for the school district you can possibly be impartial.

Facilitator: I see your point, but I have been trained to be impartial, and it certainly will not be my intention to take any sides. I'm just here to help you all.

Advocate: Well, I'm not advising my client to remain in a meeting where there is yet one more school professional to try to persuade her that she should do what's best for the school but not for the child.

Facilitator: May I just explain why my being here isn't going to take anything away from your client?

Advocate: No, you may not!

Obviously, this debate could go on for quite some time. It *might* lead the advocate to shift to a more accepting position, or it might continue to escalate and develop into a power struggle. The point is that the facilitator should not enter into debate with anyone at any time. The role of the facilitator is to support the team's collaboration toward consensus, not to argue for any position of his or her own. Debate is inherently oppositional and adversarial. There is no need for the facilitator to go there.

Having considered what *not* to do if there should be an objection to the facilitator's presence, let's now explore some recommended alternatives. Responding to objections is actually very straightforward if one just thinks back to the simple suggestion made in Chapter 2: *to be as transformative as possible and only be facilitative when the team cannot do it on its own.* How then might the facilitator use this guiding principle in responding to someone who objects? To be transformative means to assume the role of the mirror, to follow the group or the individual, and to promote recognition and empowerment. Let's see what this might look like in practice:

Advocate: Nobody told *me* you were coming!

Facilitator: So there are some concerns about my being here? [reflecting for recognition]

Advocate: Well, yes, I have some concerns.

Facilitator: How would you like to proceed? [empowerment; offering choice]

Advocate: What do you mean?

Facilitator: Well, you say you have some concerns. What would you like to do next?

Advocate: *(after uncomfortable silence)* Well, I'd like to know who invited you and what your role is.

Facilitator: Okay. *(allows the tension to just be for a moment)*

Chairperson: Mr. DeBoer, I had invited the facilitator to join us so that we could maybe have a little help in communicating well.

Advocate: But he works for the district.

Chairperson: Yes, but as he said, his role is not to take sides, just to support our collaboration.

Advocate: I don't think he can be impartial.

Facilitator: *(waits to see if anyone else will respond first; it is their meeting)* So you have some strong feelings about this. [reflecting for recognition]

Advocate: I don't want another school professional to in effect gang up on my client just to help the school get what they want.

Facilitator: Sounds like it's important that whoever assists the team be able to support all viewpoints without bias, is that it? [reframing for recognition; from negative to positive and from polarity to unity]

Advocate: Well, yes!

Facilitator: *(to team, including the parent and advocate)* So how would you all like to proceed with this issue? [empowerment]

Parent: I think he can stay. If he seems biased, we can point it out, right?

Advocate: I have my doubts, but if you want to try it. . .

Facilitator: *(looking at entire group)* Sounds like you're in agreement, then, that having a facilitator is okay provided you can point it out if bias seems to be happening, is that right? [repeating for recognition]

(Team nods in agreement and collaboration is restored.)

Is this scenario farfetched? Couldn't it, conceivably, have gone the other way? Yes, indeed. Let's see what that might look like, starting in the middle of the same scenario:

Advocate: I don't want another school professional to in effect gang up on my client just to help the school get what they want.

Facilitator: Sounds like it's important that whoever assists the team be able to support all viewpoints without bias, is that it? [reframing for recognition; from negative to positive and from polarity to unity]

Advocate: Well, yes!

Facilitator: *(to team, including the parent and advocate)* So how would you all like to proceed with this issue? [empowerment]

Parent: I think he can stay. If he seems biased, we can point it out, right?

Advocate: No. I don't want him here.

Parent: Well, you're my advocate, and I want to follow your recommendations.

Facilitator: *(looking at entire group)* Sounds like there are some differences of opinion about what would be best. [reflecting for recognition]

Chairperson: Well, some of us think it would be fine.

Facilitator: So how would you all like to proceed?

Chairperson: Well, I'm sorry to say it, but I think we'll have to honor Mr. DeBoer's preference.

Facilitator: Okay, so sounds like there's agreement that, under the circumstances, it would be best to proceed without a facilitator today, right?

(Team nods in agreement.)

Facilitator: Okay, I understand. *(leaves)*

Notice that the team members have collaborated in this decision. They have made an agreement about their disagreement, and at no point did the facilitator depart from the transformative method or from steps to ensure recognition and empowerment. Consider also that this meeting is only one facet of a much longer, ongoing journey. It may very well be that the advocate and parent will be more open to facilitation at a future meeting—an openness that might not have occurred without the "failure" of today. Trust the process! If nothing else, remember always that this is *the team's* meeting and the team's opportunity to choose. If the facilitator allows himself or herself to get too attached to the outcome, the potential for being truly neutral will be lost and he or she risks becoming just another "side" in an adversarial rather than collaborative process.

MANAGING THE MEETING

Managing the meeting is, of course, the role of the chairperson, not the facilitator. The facilitator's role at all times is to remain alert to whether collaboration is occurring and to be prepared to intervene if at any point collaboration is impaired. Some potential pitfalls in this regard are the facilitator becoming too active, being too vocal, and crossing over the line into managing rather than supporting the meeting. But what if the chairperson is not doing his or her job? Well, then the facilitator's role is not to do the job *for* him or her but to support the chairperson to manage the meeting more effectively.

Let's imagine that ground rules are not being followed and that there is considerable side talking, which the chairperson is ignoring. The facilitator must not become directive by saying, "Excuse me. I notice there is a lot of side talking going on right now." The term *side talking* is value laden and clearly implies that some team members should not be doing what they are doing. This is obviously evaluative, which is a stance the facilitator must not take.

The facilitator must also not make a veiled attempt at giving information, perhaps by saying, "I notice that not everyone is on task right now." Although this may appear to be a reflection for recognition, consider that the mirror can never reflect what it does *not* see. As a general rule, reflections are not transformative if they are phrased in the negative: "I see that no one. . . " "I notice not everyone. . . " "It seems clear than nobody is. . . " "I don't hear any. . . " The facilitator must therefore be alert to what he or she *does* see and must be prepared to reflect this in only neutral or positive terms. Thus, in the case of side talking, the facilitator could say, "I notice that several conversations are happening at the same time" (neutral) or "It seems that several people have important points that they are trying to make" (positive: "important"). If one generalization can be made about the facilitation process, it is that the facilitator will be constantly playing with words, as if silently asking himself or herself, "How can I make this thought less directive?" and "How can I make it more transformative?"

Let's consider another possibility with regard to meeting management. Imagine that one of the participants is obviously confused but the chairperson either has not noticed or is not taking any steps to address it. Obviously, collaboration cannot occur if a participant is lost, as demonstrated by his or her assuming a puzzled look or withdrawing from the conversation. Again, the facilitator cannot rightly reflect in the negative: "I notice that not everyone is following along" or "I see that several people are not participating." How, then, could these evaluative statements be phrased more transformatively? How about reflecting to the group: "I sense some confusion in the room right now" or "I see some puzzled looks." Another option, one that is generally less preferred, might be to reflect to the individual: "Mrs. Ortiz, you seem a little puzzled" or "Mr. Davis, I notice you have turned away from the table." Reflecting to the individual (rather than the group) is not inherently wrong, nor is it necessarily a departure from pure transformative method. After all, the mirror can certainly see a puzzled look or someone turning away. At the same time, consider the implications of singling out an individual, especially if that individual is the only member of the team who is not in step with the others. It may promote embarrassment and even seem critical, even if this is not the intention. Another continual challenge for the facilitator is not only to remain true to the transformative or facilitative styles but also to be very sensitive to the feelings of group members and very tactful in his or her choice of words.

Speaking of facilitative styles, the emphasis so far has been primarily on transformative interventions (recognition and empowerment), and the general recommendation has been to use these interventions *first*. But let's assume that purely transformative interventions are not working very well and now consider some additional options:

Speech pathologist: I think when we have a child on the spectrum that peer modeling in self-contained could have advantages over one-to-one.

(Parent seems lost.)

Facilitator: I sense that there may be some confusion in the room. [reflecting for recognition]

Chairperson: Well, the research clearly supports modeling by peers as a preferred intervention for children with cognitive challenges, especially if there's ADHD or AU involvement.

Facilitator: [sees the failure of the first intervention; shifts to facilitative style] My fear is that some of the terms might be confusing. Could you help me understand what you mean by *ADHD, AU, cognitive challenges, peer modeling . . . ?*

The techniques in this last intervention are facilitative, not transformative, because they lead rather than follow the group. They include sharing the conflict ("My fear is"), pointing at self, and asking for help. A detailed exploration of intervention options is presented in Chapter 5, and a summary appears in Appendix E.

WORKING WITH ADVOCATES AND ATTORNEYS

Working with advocates and attorneys raises some unique challenges. For one thing, their role is to support their client, and this *may be* at odds with supporting the collaboration of the team as a whole. Of course, this is a generalization, and there will certainly be exceptions. What is definite, however, is that the philosophy of the advocate or attorney as to *how* best to support the client will drive that person's behavior and may or may not support the vision of federal law (i.e., that IEP teams work collaboratively toward consensus in decision-making partnership).

Advocacy is not a licensed or regulated profession. Theoretically, anyone could represent himself or herself as an advocate for children in special education and possibly be invited or hired by a parent to attend a meeting in support of the IEP process. But *how* will he or she support the process? What do advocates believe their role is in this regard, and what qualifications, training, and accountability do they have to back up the influence they are likely to have on the conduct of the meeting and in the decision-making process of the parent?

It is a curious thing that, whenever the word *advocate* is mentioned among school personnel, an almost audible groan can often be heard. Many school personnel describe advocates by such nicknames as "the barracuda" or "the piranha," clearly indicating that the advocate is anything but collaborative and is instead perceived as belligerent, demanding, hostile, unpleasant, disrespectful, and so forth. School personnel have described IEP meetings that have dragged on for hours and hours, not for any particular benefit of the student but for the questions and demands of the advocate.

In all fairness, advocates can also be described in very *positive* terms. Some have considerable experience in special education and/or in raising their own children with special needs. Some have been very stabilizing influences at meetings, helping the parents to understand the IEP process and make wise decisions on behalf of the child. Some advocates have shown a strong understanding of the importance of diplomacy and collaboration and are thus able to promote these characteristics among the team as a whole. The bottom line is this: The issue is not whether advocates attend IEP meetings but rather how they behave when they get there and whether they support the vision of the law—decision-making partnership through collaboration toward consensus.

Much the same can be said about attorneys. They may attend IEP meetings with a strong commitment to collaboration and consensus or with an adversarial stance and a willingness to use position-based bargaining to ensure that their clients gets whatever thing—service, placement, reimbursement—they are seeking. A major difference, however, between attorneys and advocates is that attorneys have standardized training and qualifications—typically 4 years of college and 3 years of law school from accredited institutions, plus licensing by the state bar. They also have accountability in that they are bound to a published code of ethics and risk a grievance before the state bar if their conduct is considered unethical.

Of course, if attorneys or advocates attend IEP meetings and support collaboration through respectful communication, assuming good reason and intention, exploring interests, and so forth, then how can they be anything but a positive force at these meetings? If, in contrast, they are belligerent, disrespectful, demonizing, and locked into positions, how can they be anything but destructive? Although their attendance may be absolutely within the letter of the law, their behavior could actually be considered illegal if it violates the spirit and *intention* of the law, which is not adversity but partnership and not competition but collaboration.

If an advocate or attorney attends in support of collaboration, then the facilitator will need no additional skills and will make no additional interventions other than those that would be appropriate at *any* IEP meeting. But what if an advocate or attorney does not attend in support of collaboration? What additional skills will the facilitator require then? The answer is: none! The facilitator will not require additional skills but will only need to use the ones he or she already has. Let's consider some worst-case scenarios—the belligerent advocate or attorney who is in no way supporting collaboration toward consensus:

Chairperson: *(after introductions, ground rules, and agenda are in place)* Well, I think the first item is the review of assessments. Could I ask our diagnostician to get us started here?

Diagnostician: Well, I enjoyed working with Jamal. He stayed on task and was trying his best, so he is easy to work with. He tends to be a little intense, which I think makes it harder for him to—

Advocate: What do you mean, *intense?*

Diagnostician: Well, he seems to get frustrated if he doesn't have the answer right away.

Advocate: On what basis do you say that?

Diagnostician: Well, he just gets kind of shook up.

Advocate: Is "shook up" a new diagnosis? What qualifies you to make such a determination?

Diagnostician: *(becoming flustered)* Well, it's pretty obvious when a child is struggling and maybe taking things more seriously than—

Advocate: Please answer my question. Do you have special expertise when it comes to emotional issues? Have you studied developmental delay and how this relates to test taking in children on the autism spectrum? What training have you had in this regard?

Facilitator: *(to advocate)* Mrs. Hamilton, these seem to be important questions for you, and you must have good reasons for asking them. [reflecting for recognition and affirming *important* and *good*]

Advocate: *(ignoring facilitator's comments)* I asked a straightforward question. I would like a straight answer.

Facilitator: And if you had a straight answer it would be helpful because. . . [probing for interests]

Advocate: Don't play games with me, sir. I asked about the diag's qualifications.

Facilitator: You seem a little irritated with me. [reflecting for recognition]

Advocate: I am not irritated. I am asking a reasonable question. *(to parent)* I told you they would bring someone who would take their side.

Facilitator: *(to team)* We seem to be having a tough time right now. Any ideas what might help the team move forward on this issue? [reflecting and asking for help]

Chairperson: *(to diagnostician)* Mrs. Johansson, why don't you take a minute to share your qualifications. It's a fair question.

Diagnostician: Well, I took my undergraduate training at MSU, and then did my diag training at Western. I've been with the district 7 years but was previously with Green River Co-op for 4 years, and before that with Anderson schools.

Advocate: What training have you had in working with children on the spectrum?

Diagnostician: I have attended several state conferences on autism and quite a few in-service trainings over the years. I have also worked with many children with autism or Asperger diagnoses.

Advocate: Okay, fine. That's all I wanted to know.

Facilitator: So it sounds like the team has been able to resolve the question of qualifications, right? [reflecting for recognition]

(All nod in agreement.)

Will every confrontation like this one result in agreement? Certainly not, but notice the facilitator's responses: always remaining hopeful and positive, avoiding any semblance of alliance or judgment, avoiding entering into debate, and remaining true to the transformative and facilitative methods. The majority of the time this will be all that is required to restore collaboration— not any new or different skills, only the careful application of the skills the facilitator already has.

Now let's turn to an example of working with attorneys. In many if not most cases, an attorney for the school district will be present at an IEP meeting if a parent chooses to bring an attorney. In fact, it may be a district policy that if a parent brings an attorney, the meeting will not proceed unless the district's attorney is also present. (The reader is encouraged to clarify this point at the local level.) Let's assume that two attorneys are present at this meeting:

Chairperson: *(after introductions, ground rules, and agenda are in place)* Well, I think the first item is the review of assessments. Could I ask our diagnostician to get us started here?

Diagnostician: Well, I enjoyed working with Michael. He stayed on task and was trying his best, so he is easy to work with. He tends to be a little intense, which I think makes it harder for him to do his best, because he gets kind of shook up and can start crying or even hitting himself and calling himself names.

Chairperson: *(to parent)* Have you seen this behavior at home?

Parent's Attorney: Excuse me. As I mentioned earlier, I am here representing Mrs. Richards, and I would appreciate it if you would please address your questions and comments to me.

Chairperson: Are you saying that Mrs. Richards is not going to be sharing with us what she sees with her child at home?

Attorney: That's correct. Mrs. Richards has asked me to represent her today.

Facilitator: *(to attorney, as an uncomfortable silence befalls the group)* Mr. Hughes, I understand that you will be representing Mrs. Richards today and that questions and comments should be directed to you. You must have good reasons for this. [repeating for recognition and affirming *good* intentions]

Attorney: Well, yes, I do. My client has been intimidated, bullied, and driven to tears by these people. She is afraid to even be here without support, and I am not going to allow them to treat her in such an unprofessional fashion.

Facilitator: So it's important that your client be treated with respect and in a professional manner at school meetings, is that it? [reframing for recognition]

Attorney: No, it's that I will be speaking for her today, as I have said.

Facilitator: So there's a proposal that comments and questions be directed to Mr. Hughes. [repeating for recognition to group]

(Team responds with silence.)

Facilitator: I'm sensing some discomfort in the room right now. [reflecting for recognition]

Chairperson: I don't think this is the vision of the law at all. The purpose of the meeting is to share ideas for the benefit of the child. I don't see how a mother not even speaking is consistent with the law.

School district's attorney: Let me handle this. It's not unusual for attorneys to want to represent their clients in this way. I say we let it be okay, at least for now.

Facilitator: So there's a proposal that the team let it be okay for now. *(looks around the table)*

Chairperson: Okay, we'll see how it goes.

Facilitator: So there's an agreement that the team will conduct the meeting this way and see how it goes. [repeating for recognition]

(Team nods and collaboration is restored.)

Once again, the facilitator remains true to the recommended methods and needs no additional skills; the facilitator needs only to carefully apply the skills he or she already has. Of course, this scenario might have played out very differently. Mrs. Richards and her attorney might have gotten up and left the room, or perhaps further discussion may have led Mrs. Richards to tell her attorney that she would feel okay about participating directly, or the attorney may have independently changed his position. All of these are possible, and nothing is guaranteed. The facilitator can take great comfort in remembering that this is *the team's* meeting and that his or her goal is never to persuade anyone of anything—only to support recognition and empowerment and productive dialogue. The rest is up to the team.

5 | Strategies for Intervention

In previous chapters, transformative and facilitative interventions were discussed, and examples were presented through illustrative scenarios. It is time now to specifically enumerate 19 options, all of which have a place in the facilitator's toolbox. They can easily be organized into transformative and facilitative categories. Although they will often have elements in common, there will always be a clear and demonstrable difference: The transformative will always follow the group, much as a mirror reflects what it sees, whereas the facilitative will always lead the group, much as a supportive but not directive tour guide. Neither will tell, instruct, advise, pass judgment, or evaluate. The 19 interventions are presented below and are amplified with discussion and examples. The same list is presented again in a summary form in Appendix E for easy reference.

TRANSFORMATIVE INTERVENTIONS

The transformative interventions include a short list of only four: three for recognition (repeat, reframe, and reflect) and one for empowerment.

1. Repeat for Recognition

Repeating for recognition involves simply restating exactly what the speaker has said. Example: "Your child 'is going to remain in the general classroom no matter what.' Is that right?"

When repeating for recognition, it is important to stay close to the exact words of the speaker and to do so with an attitude of sincere respect, as if to say, "I just want to be sure I am hearing what you are saying." Note that the facilitator should avoid adding emphasis by underscoring negatives. Thus, it is of little value and possibly destructive to repeat, "You say he's a real egomaniac who doesn't care about anyone but himself." If the speaker goes on at great length and the facilitator is unable to easily repeat what was said, then repeating just a few words would be sufficient. Here is an example, with the repeated words underlined:

Speaker: My child has been at this school for 3 years, and not once have they ever sent home a report about his behavior before it gets to the point that they can't seem to handle it. Now they are saying that he is disruptive, doesn't pay attention, is often a discipline problem, and she can't manage him. This is not something that is typical of his behavior, and I feel sure that the problem is with their lack of attention to his individual needs. If they would just put him in a classroom with a teacher who cares about him and can be sensitive to his particular style of learning, I don't think he would have these challenges. He certainly didn't have them when he was in the third-grade classroom with Mrs. Johnson. They're just not willing to go the extra distance it might require to attend to his needs, and I don't think that's too much to expect of them. After all, he has rights under the law, and they are unwilling to recognize their responsibilities here.

Facilitator: He has rights under the law, and this is not typical of his behavior, is that it? [note repetition of exact words]

Repeating the speaker's exact words may be ideal, but it is not an absolute. It is enough to stay very *close* to the speaker's exact words, as the facilitator's real objective is to repeat the exact *meaning* of the words.

2. Reframe for Recognition

Reframing for recognition clarifies a feeling, perception, intention, or interest in positive terms that all can endorse. Example: "Whatever it takes, the student should have the most appropriate placement, right?"

Reframing was covered in some detail in Chapter 3. It involves taking the negative (what the speaker does not want) and restating it in the positive (what he or she does want), and taking the point out of polarity (you versus them) and restating it as a general principle that all team members are likely to endorse. Reframing can be done in one or two stages.

One-Stage Reframe

Speaker: I just don't think this child is going to do well if all he gets is support for his reading in the classroom and the parents aren't doing their part to support the process in the home.

Facilitator: Are you saying that the classroom and home environments are both important to the student's progress, and he would benefit from a unified approach?

Note that the speaker *does not* want the support to be only at school and the parents *not* to do their parts. Taking this from negative to positive means that the speaker *does* want the support to be in both locations and the parents to be doing their parts. To take this thought out of polarity (school versus parents) and into unity (whole team), the facilitator phrases it as "the classroom and home environments are both important . . . and he would benefit from a unified approach." There is no "againstness," adversity, or opposing sides in this reframe. Is it conceivable that any group member would deny that both school and home environments are important and that a unified approach would be beneficial? In reframing, the facilitator has not only promoted recognition but has also captured and redirected a torpedo of attack, highlighted a shared value and common interest, and clarified an area of agreement among all members. Collaboration is then very likely to be restored.

Two-Stage Reframe

Speaker: I just don't think this child is going to do well if all he gets is support for his reading in the classroom and the parents aren't doing their part to support the process in the home.

Facilitator: So are you saying there is a better way the student's progress can be supported? [operative words: *a better, another, a different way*]

Speaker: Well, yes.

Facilitator: And what might that be? [probing for the general principle]

Speaker: Well, the school can only do so much, and the student would benefit if the parents would support our efforts, rather than just complaining and attacking when things don't go as they expect.

Facilitator: So it sounds like you're saying that working together in a unified manner would be of greatest benefit to the child, is that it? [one-stage reframe, identifying the common value in positive terms that all members would endorse]

Speaker: Yes, exactly.

Note that, at the end of this example, the facilitator could possibly have been wrong. That is, the common principle may not have been correctly identified and the speaker might instead have said, "No that's not it." If so, the facilitator would have simply probed again, and the point for recognition would have received further clarification. For example:

Facilitator: So it sounds like you're saying that working together in a unified manner would be of greatest benefit to the child, is that it? [one-stage reframe]

Speaker: No, that's not what I meant. I mean they should stop blaming us, as though they have no contribution here.

Facilitator: So there's a better way to communicate, right? [two-stage reframe, operative words: *better way*]

Speaker: Yes. A team is only as strong as the confidence its members have in one another, and I think we deserve a little more credit and trust.

Facilitator: So trust and confidence are important for the team to do its best work for the child. [one-stage reframe]

Speaker: Right.

The facilitator need not regret having been wrong in the first reframe. The purpose of recognition is served either way, and when it comes to reframes, facilitators can make their work considerably easier by giving themselves permission to be wrong and by letting this be an integral part of the recognition process.

3. Reflect for Recognition

Reflecting for recognition involves highlighting the *process* that is observed:

- **To the group:** "There seem to be a lot of strong feelings at the moment," or "This seems to be a difficult issue for you all."

- **To the individual:** "This issue seems to be very important to you," or "Mrs. Smith, you seem perhaps a little uncomfortable."

Note that reflection differs from repeating in that no words are quoted, and it differs from reframing in that no words are rephrased. Instead, it is unspoken cues that are reflected to the team. Also, the facilitator usually has a choice as to whether to reflect to the group as a whole or to the individual. There is no categorical right or wrong in this regard. As a general principle, however, most people do not like to be singled out, especially if it is to imply an "inappropriate" behavior—such as raised voices, interrupting, side talking, and so forth. Also, some people are not comfortable getting very close to their feelings. Comments such as "You seem to be feeling very sad now" or "You are obviously very angry" may put someone on the spot. Tactfulness dictates care in the facilitator's choice of words and sensitivity in the choice of intervention. In general, facilitators should make their comments to individuals very wishy-washy, leaving plenty of room for them to avoid or deny whatever is being reflected. Thus, instead of "Wow, you are obviously very upset by what was just said," the facilitator could more safely say, "This seems to have been a little unsettling, or am I wrong?" Qualifiers, such as *might, possibly, seems, could be, sometimes, a little,* tend to soften the intensity of a communication, as do questions rather than statements; pointing at self or at the group tends to be more gentle than pointing at an individual. Again, the choice to reflect to the group rather than the individual is not an absolute—just an issue warranting awareness and sensitivity on the facilitator's part.

4. Empower

The facilitator empowers by asking questions that provide an opportunity to choose:

- **To the group:** "Where do you all want to go with that?" or "What would you all like to do next?"
- **To the individual:** "Where do you want to go with that?" or "What would you like to do next?"

In Chapter 2, it was explained that recognition and empowerment go very much hand in hand in that whenever recognition occurs, it inherently calls for choice. The wonderful saying "With awareness comes the ability to make flexible choices" is a cornerstone of Gestalt psychology. In light of this, recognition leads to choice because awareness *requires* choice—the choice to do things the same way or perhaps to make a change. Thus, reflecting that the group has strong feelings leads to the members observing their feelings and then, as a matter of course, deciding what to do next—choosing their next step.

However, there is also the process of specifically asking for a choice. Thus, if recognition by itself is not enough to motivate making a choice, the facilitator can then highlight the "choice point" more clearly. This usually takes the form of a question, such as "What would you like to do next?" or "Where would you like to go with that?" or "How would you like to proceed?" For example:

Speaker: I hate it when they say that.

Facilitator: You seem to have some strong feelings about that. [reflecting for recognition]

Speaker: You bet I do.

Facilitator: So where would you like to go with that? [empowerment]

Speaker: What do you mean?

Facilitator: Well, you say you have strong feelings. What would you like to do next? [recognition and empowerment]

Speaker: I don't know what you mean.

Facilitator: Well, what do you want to do now? [empowerment]

Speaker: I want to know why they keep saying that.

Facilitator: Okaaaay . . . [a long, hanging *okay* urges the speaker to do something more—to make a choice; empowerment]

Speaker: *(turns to chairperson)* Explain to me why you keep saying that.

In this example, recognition has led to empowerment, and empowerment has led to choice, and choice has restored collaboration as the parties now dialogue about their issues at hand. Incidentally, it is not often that a speaker has such difficulty understanding the facilitator's question of what he or she might like to do next. An example of this difficulty is included here only to suggest that it *could* happen and to show some options for the facilitator's response.

Another extremely valuable application of empowerment has to do with the issue of making agreements about disagreements. This process begins with clear recognition of the opposing views and then with the invitation for the parties to decide how they wish to proceed, which is the empowerment piece. This intervention is particularly valuable in resolving impasse, as is discussed in Chapter 6. To see what this can look like in practice, consider the following scenario:

Parent: I think he needs additional tutoring.

Teacher: I think he just needs more support at home.

Parent: You're always blaming me. It's the school's job to give him the support he needs. We're doing our part at home, believe me.

Facilitator: May I just check in to see if I'm following you? *(to parent)* Sounds like you're saying that he needs additional tutoring, and *(to teacher)* you're saying he needs more support at home. Is that right? [repeating for recognition]

(Both nod in agreement.)

Facilitator: So where would you like to go with that? [empowerment]

Teacher: Well, what if we expand the tutoring sessions from, say, 30 to 45 minutes, and the parents commit to maybe 20 minutes of bedtime reading every night?

Parent: I can go along with that.

Collaboration is restored as the parties recognize their differing perspectives and then agree on how they would like to proceed from there. They have been empowered to make agreements about their disagreements—to first clearly see their differences and then make choices accordingly.

Having covered this very short list of purely transformative interventions, let's turn now to the facilitative options. My strong recommendation is for the facilitator to strive to use transformative interventions first and to only move on to facilitative options when it is clear that the team is having difficulty restoring collaboration without additional assistance.

FACILITATIVE INTERVENTIONS

As will be evident, many of the facilitative interventions also promote recognition and empowerment. The main difference is that these lead rather than follow the group, more like a guide than a mirror.

5. Pause for Reflection

When asked to pause for reflection, the group members are thereby given a chance to consider their process. Example: "May I just touch base and ask how you all are feeling about your meeting so far?" or "Is everyone feeling like they've had a chance to speak and be heard?"

Pausing for reflection is one of the most widely applicable techniques in the facilitator's toolbox and one that fully supports the process of recognition. It can be used whenever strong feelings are evident, whenever people show signs of dissatisfaction, or whenever the team is bogged down and not making progress. The only reason it cannot be called a purely transformative intervention is, again, because it leads rather than follows the group. Once the group responds, it is very easy to return to one or more of the purely transformative options. For example:

Parent: I want my child to be allowed to bring his therapy dog to school.

Chairperson: Mr. Jenkins, as much as I'd like to honor your request, we just can't do that.

Parent: You can do it if you want to. All you need to do is show that it would help him be more focused and feel more comfortable in the classroom. It wouldn't hurt anybody at all. The dog is very well behaved. I paid $12,000 for that dog!

Teacher: Mr. Jenkins, I just can't have a dog in my classroom. Some children have allergies, and some are afraid of dogs. It wouldn't be fair to them.

Parent: I read the district policies. All you have to do is show educational benefit!

Chairperson: No, it's not that simple.

Facilitator: Excuse me just a moment. May I just ask how you all are feeling about your discussions at this point? [pausing for reflection]

Parent: This is a waste of time.

Chairperson: I think we're hitting some snags we just can't seem to get though.

Teacher: We seem to be stuck.

Facilitator: Okay. Sounds like you're struggling. [reflecting for recognition]

Teacher: I guess that's pretty obvious.

Facilitator: So where do you want to go with this? [empowerment]

Chairperson: I think we need to revisit our ground rules about being respectful and working together.

Parent: You're the ones who aren't working together.

Teacher: I think we need to remember that we're all on the same team, and we all want what's best for the child. How about we continue to talk about this, hear everybody's views, and see what we can come up with together?

Parent: Okay. So tell me why my child can't have his therapy dog in the classroom.

Chairperson: The district policy is that the only dogs allowed at school are Seeing Eye dogs for the blind. And, as Mrs. Villa mentioned, some children are afraid of dogs or have allergies. We just cannot do it even if we wanted to.

Teacher: I do have a suggestion, though. He could bring the dog to his after-school tutoring. We could meet in the covered picnic area, and I wouldn't mind at all if he has the dog with him then. How does that sound?

The team is once again collaborating, provided they are communicating, sharing ideas respectfully, and addressing their issues of common concern.

6. Ask about Ground Rules

Asking about ground rules involves inviting reflection about agreements made earlier. Example: "How are you all doing with your ground rules?"

Of course, the facilitator cannot ask the team about its ground rules if no ground rules have been set. Because they can serve as an extremely helpful safety net if difficulties arise, it is essential that establishing ground rules be part of setting the stage at the beginning of the meeting. Assuming that such rules are in place, the facilitator can at any point simply ask the team members how they see themselves doing with them. This is very similar to pausing for reflection, except that the reason for the pause is more specific: to consider the ground rules. This is entirely a move for recognition, and yet it cannot be considered purely transformative because, again, it leads rather than follows. It is therefore better categorized as a facilitative intervention.

Let's consider some different ways the facilitator might make this intervention. Two examples might be: "I notice that none of you are following your ground rules" or "I notice that some of you are not following the ground rules." Consider that both of these reflections are in the negative (*none* and *not*) and therefore contain an implied judgment that the group is doing something wrong. Whenever the facilitator feels tempted to intervene, it is always because of something that *is* being perceived, so what might that be? Perhaps that people are interrupting, raising their voices, being disrespectful, or losing focus. This, then, is what can be reflected—but in neutral or positive terms, and tactfulness is also important here. Let's consider more specifically what to say and what to avoid saying when ground rules are obviously being violated:

Avoid: "I notice that you all are not on task right now." [negative]

Avoid: "It seems that several of you are off task." [negative]

Avoid: "Wouldn't it make sense to maybe review your ground rules?" [negative]

Avoid: "I hear a lot of side talking." [evaluative, judgmental word choice]

Avoid: "Mr. Young, you seem to be raising your voice right now." [confrontational, judgmental]

Avoid: "Would it make sense to review your ground rules at this time?" [evaluative, a veiled attempt at direction]

Avoid: "I could be wrong, but would it maybe be helpful to review a few of your ground rules, or is that a bad idea?" [evaluative; although softened, it is still a veiled attempt at direction]

Consider: "I hear a number of conversations going on at the same time."

Consider: "How are you all doing with your ground rules?"

Consider: "It seems that several people are trying to make important points now."

Consider: "May I just ask if everyone is feeling comfortable with the way your meeting is going at this point?"

Consider: "There seem to be some strong feelings in the room right now."

Consider: "Mr. Young, you seem to be a little frustrated, am I right?"

The process of facilitation is as much art as science, and skilled facilitators are constantly asking themselves, "How can I make this more transformative?" "How can I make this less directive?" "How can I phrase this more positively?" and similar questions that reflect an understanding of the general principles that make for effective facilitation.

7. Hold a Focus

Holding a focus involves asking for more two times to assist in clarifying perspectives and airing feelings. Example: "Would you like to say some more about that?" (allow response) and then "Is there anything else you'd like to share about this?" (allow response).

When people have strong feelings, their emotions often interfere with positive and effective communication, as well as their ability to really listen to the perspectives of others. Yet feelings quickly dissipate when acknowledged. That is, when people can express their feelings and really be heard, the intensity of their emotions will quickly diminish. An analogy is a bathtub that quickly empties when the plug is pulled. Other familiar analogies are "venting" feelings and "getting them off your chest." In all three, the key is *moving* the feelings so that they are somehow reduced in intensity, and the best way to do this is through effective communication. Holding a focus can be especially helpful in supporting this very important process. Watch how this usually works in practice:

Parent: You are not going to keep him in the self-contained classroom!

Chairperson: But, Mrs. McKinney, we have to consider the most appropriate placement for him and also take into consideration the implications for the other children in the class.

Parent: Over my dead body! You better have a good lawyer if you do that.

Facilitator: Mrs. McKinney, you seem to have some strong feelings about this. [reflecting for recognition]

Parent: You're darn right I do.

Facilitator: Would you like to say some more about it? [holding a focus, first time]

Parent: My son has a lot of strengths that they are not even willing to consider, let alone take into account. They think that they can just move him out because they're too lazy to deal with his behaviors, but that just ain't gonna fly. I can tell you that much.

Facilitator: Anything else you might like to share about this? [holding a focus, second time]

Parent: *(less intense now)* I just want them to give him a fair chance. All kids have temper outbursts sometimes. I think they've overreacted and that there are a lot of options short of just plain removing him from the classroom.

Chairperson: So tell us some of the options you see.

Parent: Well, why couldn't we get him a one-to-one aide?

Teacher: We could maybe get a behavior specialist to observe him and help develop a behavioral intervention plan. [And now the team is collaborating once again.]

On occasion, the intensity of emotion may actually *increase* the first time that more information is requested, but with another request or even two, the intensity is sure to diminish if the person is invited to share while being given respectful attention. The initial increase is almost always because the speaker is somehow suppressing the expression of feelings the first time around, as if standing on the plug of the bathtub and not permitting it to drain.

8. Probe for Underlying Interests

Probing for underlying interests involves exploring reasons so as to gain understanding. Example: "You must have good reasons for that. Can you help the group understand your thoughts?" or "What do you see happening if you all go that route?"

The subject of underlying interests was covered in some detail in Chapter 3. Let's review a few of the governing principles that make this such an important topic.

Whenever people are asking for something, there will always be some anticipated benefit that they expect to occur if their request is granted. The expectation may or may not be realistic, but that is another matter. The point is that people only latch on to a particular idea—a thing they want—on the assumption of a future benefit. The problem is that people in negotiations are often so attached to their positions, which is to say that they are so focused on the *things,* that they may have little awareness of the end result they are expecting. Also, they often do not share that anticipated benefit with the others involved, which then makes it harder for the others to recognize it. Yet only through a thorough understanding of the anticipated benefits can the team give appropriate consideration to the good intention, show the requestor that he or she is heard and understood, and, as is usually the case, show that the end goal, or interest, is *shared.* Once these elements are in place, it will usually be so much easier for all parties to explore their options together and then be open to whatever *things* will best help them achieve their shared objectives. Because most people have never been trained in how to explore interests, the facilitator's expertise in this area may be an invaluable addition to the decision-making table. The specific words for exploring interests include variations on any of the following:

Questions that Probe for Interests

You must have good reasons for thinking this; can you share them
    with the team?

What benefits could be expected if the team did that?

How would this idea be helpful?

What do you see happening if the team were to go that route?

What would it look like if the student had that service?

What harm might come if for any reason the team did not do that?

If that request is against policy, how could the team persuade the
    principal or superintendent that an exception should be made?

Yet another very easy way to explore interests is with the hanging, incomplete sentence: "And if you did that. . . ?" Consider again the self-contained classroom dispute, presented earlier under "7. Hold a Focus":

Parent: You are not going to keep him in the self-contained classroom!

Chairperson: But, Mrs. McKinney, we have to consider the most appropriate placement for him and also take into consideration the implications of the other children in the class.

Parent: Over my dead body! You better have a good lawyer if you do that.

Facilitator: Mrs. McKinney, you must have good reasons for what you are saying. Can you share them with the team? [probing for interests]

Parent: My son has strengths that they are not taking into consideration, and if they put him in the self-contained classroom, he is never going to develop the skills he needs to be successful in a normal world.

Facilitator: So what do you see happening if he were kept in the general classroom? [again, probing for interests]

Parent: I think he would continue to model the behavior of normal kids rather than the ones with the most severe disabilities in the school.

Facilitator: And if he modeled the behavior of normal kids . . . ? [probing for interests through the incomplete sentence]

Parent: Well, take for example his speech. He has started using words that I never heard from him before because he hears them from his peers at school—such as *cool dude* and *random.* I mean it's not as if this is important vocabulary, but it shows a capacity to learn that I think he would lose if he were in the strictly special ed room.

Facilitator: So modeling for speech development is a benefit that would come from staying in the general classroom. [repeating for recognition]

Parent: Exactly. And self-esteem, too. How's he going to feel about himself if he's always put with people with serious problems? He won't have a chance of developing a healthy sense of himself.

Facilitator: So if I understand your thoughts here, it's that he would have a better chance of developing self-esteem and language skills in the general classroom, right? [again, repeating for recognition]

Parent: Yes.

Facilitator: *(to team)* So where do you all want to go with that? [empowerment]

Chairperson: I'm very concerned about the temper outbursts that he shows when he gets frustrated. The last time this happened, he threw a book across the room and hit another student, which led to a very angry phone call from her parents.

Teacher: I have 22 kids in the class and I can't be watching him closely enough at every moment. The self-contained classroom can give him much closer attention—almost one-to-one.

Facilitator: So some members see actual *benefits* in the self-contained classroom—closer attention, less risk to others. [repeating for recognition]

Parent: I can see the need to protect the other children. If someone threw a book at my son, I'd be pretty steamed about it, too. I just don't think removing him is the only option.

Facilitator: There may be other options. [reframing for recognition]

Parent: *(to team)* Yes. There must be *something* else.

Special education teacher: What if we do a behavioral assessment and maybe have a partition in the classroom until we get the information we need to make a final determination?

(All indicate a willingness to try this first.)

Note that the facilitator has explored the interests of all sides of the discussion and in so doing has helped the team members to see that they *all* share an interest in the child's self-esteem, in his language development, in classroom management, and in sufficient individualized attention. Their disagreement is not over their interests but over the best *options* for addressing these interests. As the members *recognize* their interests and see that they are shared, they will usually become more open to considering other options. Without support in the exploration of their interests, however, team members would probably remain locked into inflexible positions, demonizing those who disagree, and escalating their dispute—possibly into a costly due process hearing or formal complaint that may have been easily avoided.

9. Acknowledge

To acknowledge is to recognize a possible situation, feeling, or thought. Example: "Mrs. Jones, some of those suggestions must be really hard to hear" or "So much information can sometimes be kind of overwhelming."

Acknowledging is a way of showing recognition for the feelings or circumstances of one or more of the team members. It has much in common with reflecting for recognition, but if it adds to what the mirror sees or if it leads rather than follows, it is better placed in the facilitative list of options. It can also be very helpful because of the supportive nature of the intervention.

When people feel troubled or unhappy, what often makes the burden lighter is to know that someone understands what they are going through—that someone can see things from their point of view. This, of course, is the process of recognition. What also seems to be true is that the more fully people can "stand in their truth," the more easily they can take their next steps forward, and the more fully others can accept people just to be where they are, the more easily they can move on to whatever is next for them. Thus, when people are allowed to feel their anger and are supported to do so, they usually move very quickly out of the anger and into another feeling. The more fully people can be supported to feel their sadness or loss, the more easily they can move forward toward feeling something else. This is simply because human emotions are dynamic rather than static, always pushing for expression and release, although they can also be suppressed and their movement obstructed. Much like water in a plugged tub, the energy of emotions can be "bound" and may not move at all.

Just as open communications and the acknowledgment of unpleasant feelings tend to move emotions, suppression and avoidance tend to hinder their movement, and negative thinking and inflexible behavior styles tend to perpetuate them. Of course, a detailed discussion of emotions belongs in the domain of psychology rather than facilitation, and yet it is enough to recognize the simple fact that effective communication helps people who feel bad to feel better very quickly, and the support of others can assist this process in powerful ways. Most of the tools in the facilitator's toolbox offer this kind of support. This is illustrated in the following scenario, in which the changing emotion is the key issue to observe:

Parent: I just don't believe this! She is not "emotionally disturbed." How can you even say that? She just needs a little support. What is wrong with you people? [very angry]

Facilitator: That term was really hard to hear, wasn't it? [both reflecting for recognition and acknowledging]

Parent: Well, yes. She's *not* disturbed. She's sensitive, and that's what's so beautiful about her. But they don't even see that. [still angry now but less so]

Facilitator: Sounds like there are some things the team could be seeing more clearly, right? [acknowledging; also part of a two-stage reframe in probing for something different the team could see]

Parent: Right. I want them to see how special she is. *(tears)* She just gets easily frustrated, that's all. [expresses sadness more than anger now]

Teacher: Mrs. Larson, I want you to know that I think she *is* very special. I like working with her. I just can't manage her behavior sometimes. It's just too much for me.

Diagnostician: When I said *emotionally disturbed*, that's just a label we have to use to establish eligibility. It's not that she isn't a great kid. She *is* sensitive, and she *is* beautiful. You're absolutely right.

Parent: *(crying)* She's a great kid. I want you to know she's a great kid. [expresses grief]

The point of this example is not to show a successful outcome but only to illustrate how emotions change in response to clear communication and the support received. Acknowledgment and recognition go a long way toward providing such support.

10. Affirm

Affirming involves the use of praise or agreement as a means of support. Example: "I can see that you are very committed to your child's education."

Affirmation is similar to acknowledgment but differs to the extent that it adds a positive spin, as if to praise the speaker in some way. Although this may seem a small departure from acknowledgement, it is a clear departure from the transformative method: A good mirror reflects what is and does not add any spins. But isn't it evaluative to add a positive spin? The answer to this important question is that affirming is evaluative of the *process* and is used to support whatever promotes collaboration. Affirming provides no evaluation, positive or negative, about the *content* of the team's discussion. In a sense, the facilitator's role, expertise, and contribution to the meeting are that he or she is a champion of collaboration. Whatever supports the team's collaborative process is good, great, wonderful, outstanding; the content and specifics, however, are none of his or her business.

Let's compare and contrast some of the positive things a facilitator might say, because what exactly he or she affirms is of critical importance and ultimately determines if he or she remains true to the facilitative method or crosses the line into the evaluative and directive style.

Avoid: "That's an important point you've raised." [evaluative: praising what was said, which is content rather than process]

Consider: "There's an important point you're trying to make." [facilitative: affirming the speaker's desire to share a point that is important to *him,* process not content]

Avoid: "There are good reasons for additional testing." [evaluative: content]

Consider: "You must have good reasons for saying that." [facilitative: assuming good reason and intention, which is an important element of collaborative *process*]

Avoid: "Your point about behavior management is well taken." [evaluative: content]

Consider: "You phrased that very well." [facilitative: affirming the clear communication, which, again, is process, not content, and an important element of collaboration]

Avoid: "You've really developed a great IEP." [evaluative: content]

Consider: "You've done great work today—real collaboration." [facilitative: process]

11. Refocus

Refocusing involves gently leading a participant back to the issue at hand. Example: "Could I ask you to summarize the key points you'd like the group to understand about this?"

Refocusing is yet another facilitative approach that has everything to do with recognition, asking the speaker to clarify what he or she is trying to say. Again, however, because it leads rather than follows, it is better categorized as facilitative rather than transformative. Refocusing is particularly valuable when the speaker is long winded and the points being made are difficult to see. Although this basic strategy may need little explanation, an example might be of value in highlighting some of the subtleties.

Chairperson: *(to diagnostician)* So, Mrs. Mueller, can you share with us the results of the testing you did and whether it suggests that eligibility is still appropriate?

Diagnostician: When I tested Anna, she was really a pleasure to work with. She tried her best at all times, although she was shy and really quiet most of the time. I think she is clearly still eligible. She shows what I think is a specific learning disability, with a pronounced discrepancy between her ability and academic functioning in both written and oral expression. I see her functioning within the average range of cognitive ability while demonstrating relative strength in auditory processing skills; however, she is more than 2 years below age and grade level in several areas. My greatest concern is the severe expressive language processing deficit and the lag in visual perception processing that are clearly affecting her academic skills. These are not primarily attributable to unfamiliarity with the English language, although that may be a minor factor. I just don't think it's the real issue for her.

Teacher: Can you say that again? I think you lost me with some of the terminology.

Diagnostician: Well, like I say, I think it's a specific learning disability. She's got some issues with language, but that's not enough to explain it. Cognition and auditory skills are strong for her, but I'm looking at the widening discrepancy from peers, which seems to be 2 years now, when it was more like 1 year the last time I tested her—a year ago. It's the language component and visual perception that have me most concerned. In fact, I think that's really what we're looking at here.

Facilitator: *(to diagnostician, observing puzzled looks and sensing confusion)* Wow, you have really put a lot of effort into that report and have so much information to share. [affirming the effort, not the content] Could I ask you to summarize the key points the team needs to understand right now? [refocusing]

Diagnostician: Well, she has strengths but is falling more and more behind, and the profile suggests an SLD, which I think is what we have to use in making our determination.

Facilitator: SLD. [repeating for recognition]

Diagnostician: Specific learning disability.

Facilitator: So you're saying that the student has a specific learning disability, and that's why she is still eligible for special education services, is that it? [repeating for recognition]

Diagnostician: Yes.

12. When in Doubt, Check It Out

If a possible situation warrants confirmation, ask. Example: "Mr. Worczyk, are you maybe a little upset right now?" or "How are you feeling about that suggestion?"

As with several other facilitative interventions, "checking it out" serves to directly promote recognition, but what makes it different from reflecting is that it leads rather than follows—something more characteristic of a guide than a mirror. Most of the time, a simple reflection (so as to "make it more transformative") will be sufficient to achieve the facilitator's goal, and yet there may be times when a little added emphasis may be helpful. This intervention may be especially useful when the speaker's words, tone, or body language are not easy to read. Here's an example:

Teacher: I think additional tutoring is not the answer here. The real question isn't the time frame but whether or not the work that we're doing with the student is really designed to meet his needs.

Chairperson: I think what you're saying makes good sense.

Parent: No, it doesn't.

Chairperson: Tell us why it doesn't.

Parent: Thirty minutes once a week isn't making a dent. He needs more, and you don't want to do it because you just don't want to free up the time. Tell the truth.

Chairperson: If we really felt he needed it, we would do it.

(Parent sulks.)

Facilitator: I sense some tensions in the room. [reflecting for recognition]

Parent: No, I'm okay with it. Let's just move on.

Facilitator: *(unsure if the parent is really comfortable at this point)* Are you maybe a little irritated, or are you comfortable with where things are now? [when in doubt, check it out]

Parent: Well, there's nothing to be gained by arguing with them. They're gonna do whatever they want no matter what I say.

Chairperson: Mrs. Waggoner, that's not true. We are very interested in your thoughts and opinions. Can't we sometimes respectfully disagree?

Parent: You say that, but every suggestion I make you discount.

Although this conversation will continue, it is enough for now to see how the check it out option might fit and to notice that the team members are now collaboratively discussing how they communicate—whether they are welcoming thoughts and opinions and considering the issue of respectful disagreement.

Let's return to the facilitator's last intervention in the preceding example. If, instead, of saying "there's nothing to be gained," the parent had repeated her position of "let's just move on," a skilled facilitator would honor her request, because recognition and empowerment would have been clearly offered and a choice would have been clearly made. Even if the facilitator firmly believes it is not a wise decision or that the parent's statement is not even true, that is *not* for him or her to say. To do anything *other* than honoring the parent's decision at such a point would be to become directive, implying that the choice the parent has made is wrong.

13. Ask for Help

Ask the individual or the team for options or suggestions. Example: "What could the group do to be most helpful to you right now?" or (to the team) "What might help you all move forward at this point?"

Asking for help serves to raise recognition by clarifying options available to the team, and it supports empowerment by presenting new choices. It must be considered facilitative because it leads rather than follows. As an example:

(Team is silent and seems to be stuck.)

Facilitator: Looks like you've reached a hard spot in your discussions. [reflecting for recognition]

Parent: This meeting is going nowhere.

Chairperson: We just seem to be spinning our wheels.

Facilitator: Spinning wheels. [repeating for recognition]

Chairperson: Right.

Parent: I can agree on that.

Facilitator: So what do you all want to do next? [empowerment]

Chairperson: I don't think there's really anything we can do.

Parent: I'm ready to go home.

Teacher: I need to get back to my class.

Facilitator: *(seeing that the transformative intervention has not enough restored collaboration)* Well, what do you think might help you all move forward at this point? Anyone have any suggestions? [asking for help]

Chairperson: I think we need to have more open minds and be willing to consider different views.

Parent: I think they need to be willing to see my child's strengths and not just her weaknesses.

Teacher: We also need to be aware of the time. I only have 10 minutes before my substitute has to leave.

Facilitator: So let me see if I follow you. Open minds, recognizing strengths, and watching the time—these are what I'm hearing you all say would be helpful. [repeating for recognition]

Parent: Yeah, but that goes both ways.

Facilitator: It's important that all team members be open, see the strengths, and watch the time, is that what you mean? [one-stage reframe]

Parent: Exactly.

Chairperson: *(to parent)* Well, I'm certainly willing to consider your thoughts and acknowledge Bobby's strengths Mr. Donaldson. And *(to teacher)* let me ask the principal if she can arrange some additional class coverage for you. [And the team is collaborating once again.]

The great value of facilitative options is that they provide possibilities that the team members may not have thought of on their own. To rigidly adhere to a purely transformative model can lead to failures of collaboration that need not occur. Some proponents of the transformative approach might argue that there is much more room for the use of such so-called facilitative options within the transformative model and contend that the transformative facilitator *can* move in such directions. The main difficulty with such an argument, however, is that the lines that define the transformative model then become somewhat blurred, which makes the method very difficult to teach or learn. Because both the transformative and facilitative models are considered entirely appropriate within the philosophy being endorsed in this book, the issue becomes somewhat academic and of limited practical value. Again, simply stated, the recommendation is for the facilitator to use transformative interventions first and to use facilitative options when the team members are struggling to respond effectively on their own.

14. Apologize

Apologizing is a way to recognize a possible wrongdoing, even when it may not be the facilitator's fault. Example: "I am really sorry if I've been taking their side. I apologize for whatever I may have done to give that impression."

Giving an apology is probably one of the least frequently used of the facilitator's interventions, but it does have its place. It may be the most appropriate response when any participant accuses the facilitator of wrongdoing, even if the facilitator does not believe he or she has made an error. When apologies are used, it is recommended that they be followed by *I* rather than *you, they, he,* or *it.* As examples:

Avoid: "I'm sorry you see me that way."

Avoid: "I'm sorry if you think I have been taking their side."

Avoid: "I'm sorry you all are in this situation now."

Avoid: "I'm sorry they didn't seem to hear what you were saying."

Avoid: "I am sorry if it seemed like your thoughts weren't important."

Consider: "I am sorry for whatever I may have said to give that impression."

Consider: "I am sorry for interrupting you."

Consider: "I am sorry if I appeared insensitive to your feelings."

Consider: "I'm sorry—I'm not following you on this point."

Consider: "I'm sorry if what I said was out of place."

Consider: "I'm sorry I wasn't more clear in what I meant to say."

What is absolutely essential is that, if the facilitator says "I'm sorry," it must be said with real sincerity. Positive communicating and setting a good example are among the essential roles of the facilitator, and being sincere is an integral part of both of these.

15. Make a Deal

Making a deal involves asking the other party or parties to agree to speak up if they perceive a certain behavior or have a negative feeling. Example: "Mr. Green, if you see me taking sides, would you be willing to point it out and let me know?"

This technique proposes that an agreement be made to highlight and bring recognition to an issue the next time it appears. It is an extremely helpful response to an accusation of one team member against another or, potentially, against the facilitator. It is inherently collaborative in that it requires the group members to work together, and it stands in marked contrast to the common but less helpful response of contradiction. In contradicting, one party defends or denies the allegations of another, which is inherently adversarial and implies that one person is right and the other is wrong. Some brief sample dialogues will illustrate these alternative responses to an accusation. Notice that the same three scenarios are repeated, and only the response changes.

Contradiction

Parent: *(to teacher)* You don't like working with my child, and you didn't want him in your classroom to begin with.

Teacher: Yes, I do, and I did want him in my classroom. I was open to having him there. It's just that his behaviors have turned out to be more than I had expected.

Teacher: *(to parent)* You are not doing your part to support the team's process. It would help if you would try and be more of a team player.

Parent: That's not true. I *am* a team player—just as much as anyone else.

Parent: *(to chairperson)* You say I'm an important part of the team, but whatever I say, you either ignore or tell me it's not a good idea.

Chairperson: Mrs. Jones, you *are* an important part of the team. It's just that not everything you propose is necessarily a workable response to the solution.

Making a Deal

Parent: *(to teacher)* You don't like working with my child, and you didn't want him in your classroom to begin with.

Teacher: Mr. Anderson, if at any time I seem to not like your child, could you point that out so I can see what I did to give that impression?

Teacher: *(to parent)* You are not doing your part to support the team's process. It would help if you would try and be more of a team player.

Parent: If I do anything to suggest I am not supporting the team's process, can you help me see right then and there what I am doing to make it seem that way?

Parent: *(to chairperson)* You say I'm an important part of the team, but whatever I say, you either ignore or tell me it's not a good idea.

Chairperson: Mrs. Gianelli, if you see me ignoring you or telling you that your ideas are not good ones, can you point that out to me so I can see what I may be saying or doing to appear that way?

In these three examples of making a deal, the response has not been contradiction but rather openness to the possibility of what is alleged and an invitation to promote recognition by calling attention to it at the moment in question. Because the team members may not already have this skill in their toolboxes, it is something the facilitator can sometimes offer, with great benefits. It is especially appropriate as a response to any accusations made to the facilitator. It may be useful at other times as well. Consider these examples:

Making a Deal: Advocate and Facilitator

Advocate: *(to facilitator)* It's so obvious that you are on their side—the only time you speak up and say anything is to praise them for something they said.

Facilitator: [starts out transformative] Sounds like there's a better way I could be communicating. [two-stage reframe, instead of "No, I'm not" or "That's not true"]

Advocate: Well, for one thing, you could see the benefit of some of the comments my client and I make, too.

Facilitator: So it's important that all views are given appropriate respect and consideration, is that what you mean? [one-stage reframe]

Advocate: Yes, exactly.

Facilitator: *(to advocate and parent)* Would you be willing to call me on it right then and there if I seem to be failing to show respect to the views of any team members? That would really help me to see what I might be doing to give that impression. [making a deal]

Making a Deal: Teacher and Parent

Teacher: *(to parent)* I think you have to be open to differing viewpoints and not just assume that if we don't accept your idea that it means we don't value your opinions.

Parent: I *am* open to differing viewpoints. You just think that anyone who sees things differently is being closed minded. [contradiction]

Teacher: I don't see you as closed minded. I just think you need to consider the reasons for things I am suggesting. [contradiction]

Parent: Of course you think I'm closed minded. Why else would you be saying I need to be open to different viewpoints? [contradiction]

Facilitator: May I interrupt here just for a moment? Sounds like you both have some important points you are trying to make. [reflecting for recognition and affirming *important*]

Parent: Yeah, but she's not hearing me.

Teacher: I *am* hearing you!

Facilitator: Sounds like you both feel it's important that everyone at the table be heard, am I right? [one-stage reframe; although the facilitator uses *you* or *you both,* the principle is held in unity—*everyone at the table*]

(Parent and teacher both nod in agreement.)

Facilitator: So where would you like to go with that? [empowerment]

Parent: Well, she should be more willing to listen to what I have to say.

Teacher: Mr. Shepherd, I do listen to what you have to say!

Parent: No, you don't. You just tell me why it isn't right or a good idea.

Teacher: That's just not true.

Facilitator: [seeing that the pure transformative is not enough] May I just ask a question? Sounds like you both share a value in open minds and listening to ideas even when you disagree, am I right? [reflecting for recognition]

(Both nod in agreement.)

Facilitator: What would you think about this idea—and tell me if you think it's off the mark, okay? Would it make sense to maybe point out to each other right then and there if you see the other person being closed minded and not open to ideas? Could that be helpful, maybe, so you could see what is happening to give the impression that it seems neither one of you wants to be giving? What would you think about that? [making a deal]

Teacher: Okay, I'm willing to try that.

Parent: Sure, why not?

Notice the appropriately wishy-washy way in which the facilitator has presented the proposal. The reason is simple: so that all power remains with the parties and they can freely say *yes* or *no.* Consider how very much more forceful and even directive it might have sounded had the facilitator said more bluntly, "What if you point out to each other right then and there if you see the other person being closed minded and not open to ideas?" Very similar words, but very different music!

16. Play with the Time Shape

Playing with the time shape involves proposing a short-term solution to be reevaluated later. Example: "What would you think about maybe trying this idea for, say, a month or so, and then, if it isn't going well, maybe change it at your next meeting?"

Playing with the time shape can be an extremely valuable intervention, all the more so because the parties themselves may not have thought of it. The facilitator who draws this card can thus add a helpful possibility for the team to consider. This option is based on the very simple observation that people are usually more willing to agree to a short-term solution that has a doorway out than to something they will be locked into much more permanently. The following example is based on a real-life facilitated IEP meeting and is actually the same scenario with which Chapter 1 began. The main difference is that, as presented in Chapter 1, there was no facilitator present and thus no one to support the group members with interventions they may not have thought of on their own.

Speech therapist: I think your son would benefit from some time in the general classroom so he can model the speech of his peers.

Parent: Well, his doctor said he should have one-to-one therapy, so I don't want to agree to that.

Speech therapist: But there are things he will gain from his peers that just aren't the same one-to-one with an adult.

Parent: Well, I'm not going to agree to something that is not what his doctor recommended.

Facilitator: So may I just check in and see if I'm understanding what you're saying? Would that be okay?

(Both nod.)

Facilitator: *(to parent)* Sounds like you're saying that the doctor made a recommendation and you don't want to go against that, is that right? [repeating for recognition]

Parent: Yes. That's right.

Facilitator: *(to speech therapist)* And you're saying that there are benefits that Andre would receive in the classroom that he can't get in one-to-one services with an adult, is that right?

Speech therapist: Right. They learn a lot from their peers.

Facilitator: Well, what would you think about maybe trying him in the general classroom for maybe a week or two and seeing how it goes? Then, if it doesn't seem to be a good idea, you could meet once again and reconsider. How does that sound? Any value in an idea like that? [playing with the time shape]

Parent: *(after a brief pause)* Okay. We can try it. But *(to speech therapist)* would you come with me to his next doctor's appointment so you can explain this to the doctor?

Speech therapist: Sure. I can do that.

This is based on a true story, and there were no ripples of tension, anger, or conflict. The disagreement was very quickly and easily bridged by the facilitator using the play with the time shape intervention. The facilitator *might* have reached for a simple empowerment response ("Where would you like to go with that?") but chose to be more facilitative because it seemed unlikely that the team would consider this simple solution on their own, and, if perhaps they could have, it might have taken a lot of time to get there. It was a judgment call on the part of the facilitator, and yet that is what the facilitation process is all about: the facilitator knowing the options at his or her disposal and using professional judgment as to when to use which, and why. Consider also that this scenario could easily have escalated, as portrayed in Chapter 1, and, in fact, the parent had been described as extremely difficult, which is why facilitation had been requested. But in reality, there was nothing difficult about her. She was just trying to look out for the best interests of her child, as any reasonable parent would do, and did not want to go against her doctor's advice—again, something very understandable.

The question might easily arise about whether proposing that the team consider playing with the time shape isn't directive. After all, isn't the facilitator implying that the right answer is to try something for a brief period to see how it goes? Let's review two elements that have a bearing on this very important question.

First, the facilitative model does allow the facilitator to participate in option generation. The analogy is the travel guide who can offer a suggestion for the group to consider, provided that the group is completely free to accept or reject it. A close look at the facilitator's words in this example shows that such freedom is clearly provided: "Well, *what would you think* about *maybe* trying him in the general classroom for *maybe* a week or two and seeing how it goes? Then, if it doesn't seem to be a good idea, you could meet once again and reconsider. *How does that sound? Any value in an idea like that?*" Notice the questions and qualifiers that provide easy opportunities for the team members to say no. Note also that the facilitator has not proposed a solution; he has only raised the possibility of a time arrangement for a suggestion that a *team member* has proposed (i.e., to place the student in the general classroom).

A second consideration is this: If the facilitator *can* participate in option generation, couldn't he or she theoretically make specific suggestions, such as getting additional testing, checking the research literature, asking advice from the director of special education, looking into the district policies, providing additional services, changing the placement, or any of a long list of options the team may not yet have considered? The answer emerges when one remembers the purpose of the transformative and facilitative models, which is to encourage the team to collaborate and to draw out its own wisdom rather than foster any dependence on the facilitator. In general, if the facilitator keeps looking *to the team* for suggestions, it should very rarely be necessary to offer *any* content possibilities. At the same time, it may not be categorically wrong to do so, if and only if they are presented at the facilitator's wishy-washy best, giving the team members full freedom to accept or reject them as they wish. As mentioned in Chapter 2, "skilled facilitative facilitators always recognize that their options fall along a continuum and would choose first to maximize the self-direction of the team, reserving their more active contribution for when the team members cannot do it on their own" (p. 21). Also, as discussed in Chapter 6, some facilitation programs take a firm stance on this subject, requiring that their facilitators do not at any time participate in option generation when it comes to the content of the team's discussions. Again, the need to do so should rarely arise if the facilitator uses the *process* interventions available. Also, if there *is* such a governing policy, then the facilitator should know what this means and accept that a line has been clearly drawn.

17. Share Your Good Intention

Sharing your good intention involves explaining why you are saying what you are. Example: "I really want you to feel safe to express your thoughts and feelings, Mrs. Nakamura."

The very simple act of verbalizing a good intention can be a powerful way of showing support, and the members seated around the table will *always* have good intentions. It seems to be inherent in human nature to mean well, even when the behaviors people might choose for expressing those intentions are not the best and may even be later regretted.

The probability is high that IEP teams in conflict and disagreement will see and show a preponderance of negative feelings and negative thoughts and that positive comments, feelings, and intentions will be less frequently verbalized. The facilitator can help elicit these positives from the group members by using an intervention presented earlier, probing for interests, by asking such affirming questions as "You must have good reasons for thinking this; can you share them with the group?" He or she could even go so far as to say, "You must have a good intention behind that suggestion; what might that be?"

It was mentioned in Chapter 3 that among the roles of the facilitator are to set a good example and to promote positive communication. One way to do this while showing support for the team members is for the facilitator to verbalize his or her own good intentions. In counseling practice, this has been called the *use of self,* when "I" statements referring to the *counselor's* experience can help to raise awareness and empower the client by providing opportunities to make new and different choices. Let's see how this particular form of the use of self, sharing a good intention, can empower the team members to choose:

Parent: You're not willing to listen to anything I say.

Teacher: Yes, we are. We just don't always agree that the things you are asking for are best.

Parent: Just forget it.

Facilitator: Looks like you all have hit a hard spot. [reflecting for recognition]

Parent: Well, it's obvious nobody cares what I think anyway, so why bother?

Facilitator: Mr. Abernathy, I know *I* care what you think. I want you to feel welcome to share your thoughts and feelings. [sharing the good intention]

Parent: Well, maybe you do, but they don't.

Facilitator: So is there anything the team could do to be more responsive? Do you have any suggestions that could help the other members show that they care? [asking for help]

Parent: Well, for one thing, I don't always need for them to agree with me.

Facilitator: *(noticing he did not answer the question)* And how could the members show that they do care what you think? [asking for help by repeating the question]

Parent: Well, if I propose something for my son, it's because I think there's a value in it.

Facilitator: There's a value in it. [repeating for recognition]

Parent: And they could at least consider it.

Facilitator: So when someone raises a point or makes a suggestion, the team could at least consider the idea. Is that what you mean? [reframing for recognition]

Parent: Yes. I'll do it for them.

Facilitator: So there's a proposal that the team be willing to consider the views that are offered by its members. [repeating for recognition] Where do you all want to go with that? [empowerment]

(All indicate agreement.)

The purpose of this example is to show how sharing the good intention of the facilitator may be a helpful step in the dialogue. It is not likely to be used in isolation, and we can readily see the use of additional interventions that have led the group to a place of agreement: repeating, reflecting, reframing, empowering, and asking for help.

18. Point at Self

By pointing at self, any perceived ignorance or impatience can be directed at the facilitator in order to avoid putting anyone else in an uncomfortable position. Example: "I'm not sure I am following you, Mr. Kumar."

Pointing at self is another example of the "use of self" and is particularly applicable when the facilitator notices a lot of acronyms and professional jargon that may leave other members in the dark. Instead of confronting the speaker, the group, or the listener, the facilitator can be the one who is lost or confused. The same intervention can be used if someone seems angry or frustrated with another person at the table. The following are some examples of what a facilitator might or might not say:

Avoid: "Mrs. Martinez, could I just ask if you are following what the diagnostician was saying?" [checking it out, but this may put the listener in the awkward position of having to either confess that she is lost and perhaps feel foolish or deny being lost even when she is]

Avoid: "Dr. Smith, I wonder if you might be able to say that again in a more user-friendly way?" [evaluative, implying that Dr. Smith has done something wrong]

Avoid: "Team, I notice a lot of jargon and acronyms being used." [reflecting for recognition but evaluative, implying that the team should not be doing this]

Consider: "I'm not sure I'm following. Could I ask you to explain that for me, please?" [pointing at self]

Avoid: "Mr. Ling, you seem very frustrated with Mrs. Goldberg right now." [reflecting for recognition, but underscoring polarity—him against her]

Avoid: "Mr. Ling, you seem very frustrated right now." [reflecting for recognition, but singling him out in a way that may put him in an uncomfortable position]

Avoid: "Team, some of you seem to be having a little trouble understanding what is being said, am I right?" [reflecting for recognition, but this may put some members in an awkward position]

Consider: "Mr. Ling, you seem to have an important point you are trying to express. Could you help me understand your thoughts or concerns?" [pointing at self]

19. Redirect (Draw the Fire)

Redirecting involves asking that the conversation be directed to the facilitator as a means of reducing the intensity toward a member of the team. Example: "Mr. Benik, may I interrupt you? Could I ask you to tell me more about that?"

Redirecting is another example of the use of self. It is particularly valuable when one member is attacking another and can be used to "pull the speaker off" the other person by shifting his or her focus to the facilitator. As a result, the speaker's "fire" is likely to diminish considerably, as he or she is angry not at the facilitator but rather at another individual on the team. One of the goals of redirecting is for the speaker to make eye contact with the facilitator, and the facilitator will want to try and ensure that this occurs. To *not* redirect this level of emotion is to risk continued intense and unpleasant verbal attacks from one member to another. Here is what this intervention might look like in practice:

Parent: (*to chairperson*) I am *not* going to let you keep my daughter in *that* teacher's classroom.

Chairperson: I think a behavioral assessment in that classroom could give us—

Parent: No! No way! I told you, and I'm going tell you one more time, it is not going to happen!

Facilitator: Mr. Connor, you seem to have strong feelings about this issue. [reflecting for recognition]

Parent: *(still looking and pointing at chairperson)* I told you I am not going to let you keep my child in that teacher's classroom. And if you think you are, well, you better get ready for some things you aren't going to like to see [implying legal action] because I'll be dead in my grave before I let you do that!

Facilitator: Mr. Connor. I can see this is an important issue for you, and I would like to understand it better. [sharing the good intention] May I ask you to help me understand your thoughts? [asking for help] Could you tell *me* more about it? [redirecting]

Parent: *(still to chairperson)* You're just not hearing me, are you? I said *no* and I mean *no*!

Facilitator: Mr. Connor. Mr. Connor, it would really help me if you could talk to *me* about this. [pointing at self] Would you be willing to talk to me for just a moment? [redirecting]

Parent: *(now to facilitator)* They just don't hear a darn thing I say. I tell them again and again, but they just won't hear it.

Facilitator: I can see this is really important to you, and I really want to be respectful of your ideas, Mr. Connor. [reflecting for recognition and sharing the good intention] Can you help me understand why that might be? [pointing at self and asking for help]

Parent: *(to facilitator)* My son comes home every day crying about the way that teacher treats him. She is always putting him down and embarrassing him in front of the other kids, and they then tease him mercilessly for the rest of the day. I'm not going to let this go on.

Facilitator: I can see you really care about your son's well-being. [affirming]

Parent: Well, of course I do. Wouldn't you if it were your child?

Facilitator: So it's important that a child have a safe environment when he's at school, is that what you mean? [reframing]

Parent: Obviously.

Facilitator: So if he were moved to a different classroom, there could be some benefits, is that what you're saying? What might they be? [probing for interests]

Parent: Well, he would have a clean start with kids who don't tease him all the time and with a teacher who knows how to manage her classroom.

Facilitator: Your son should be safe and treated with respect in a classroom where there is discipline and order, is that it? [reframing]

Parent: And with a teacher who is competent!

Facilitator: And with staff who are qualified and use appropriate interventions? [reframing]

Parent: Exactly.

Facilitator: *(to team)* Okay, so anyone have any ideas what might move you all forward? [asking for help]

Of course, this discussion could continue, and it may be that no agreement is reached. It is likely, however, that once the parent sees that his points are being heard and that the group recognizes his interests, collaboration toward a successful resolution will now take place. After all, the source of the parent's intense anger was clearly stated: He does not believe the team is hearing what he has to say. That he is locked into a single position (removal to another classroom) is not surprising. It is an American cultural standard of negotiation to fight for the things we say we want, believing that we appropriately and rightfully champion the causes of our children in doing so. With the facilitator's interventions, as shown in this example, the probability, but not certainty, exists that other options will be considered or that the group will agree that the parent's request is appropriate.

The point of this scenario is to show how important it can be for the facilitator to redirect the intensity of the speaker. Without the facilitator drawing this fire, the speaker might otherwise be truly abusive to other team members, even if motivated by the best of intentions. When it comes to hostility and abuse, nothing is more antithetical to collaboration or more destructive to the continued benefits of the meeting. Although some school administrators might be quick to end the meeting as soon as a participant becomes enraged, there are downsides to doing so unless it is absolutely necessary. The child's IEP is still not in place, the time of all who have prepared for and perhaps traveled to this meeting is wasted, an additional meeting will have to be scheduled, feelings will be hurt, the team's working relationships for the future will be damaged, and the possibility of escalation into legal action is high. For all of these reasons, the facilitator's use of redirection can often serve as a much-needed alternative.

DIRECTIVE INTERVENTIONS: DO NOT ENTER!

Before concluding this chapter on strategies for intervention, it may be helpful to summarize some of the common pitfalls of new facilitators and to urge caution against using them:

- Instructing/explaining: "Well, under district policy . . ."
- Giving advice or expert opinion: "In my opinion, you should . . ."

- Telling: "Team, you need to remember your ground rule about . . . "
- Wolves in sheep's clothing (veiled attempts at giving information): "Do you think reviewing your ground rules would be a good idea about now?" "I can't tell you what to do, but doesn't the law have some language about that?" "Wouldn't it make sense to get some more testing?"

EXERCISES IN IDENTIFYING INTERVENTION OPTIONS

What follows are a few examples of what a facilitator might say at an IEP meeting. You might like to see if you can identify the interventions being demonstrated. Note that these are not necessarily ideal interventions, and as an additional step, you might like to critique the words being used and propose a better way of responding to the same situation. Answers and discussion appear in Appendix F.

1. "I'm feeling a little lost. When you say 'he only cares about the money,' is it that you're not trusting the real motivation? Can you help me understand what you mean here?"

2. "There seem to be some strong feelings right now. I hear a lot of interruptions and a few choice words. Anyone else seeing that?"

3. "Say some more about that. This seems to be a very important issue for you, and I want to be sure I understand where you're coming from."

4. "Mr. Harris, I'm not really comfortable with the way that was said. I know you have an important point you are trying to make. Could you say it again, please, without the swear words?"

5. "This seems to be really hard for you, so what would you like to do next? Would you like to maybe take a break? Could a break maybe be helpful at this point?"

6. "Team, I'm sorry to interrupt you. Just wanted to check in and see how we are feeling about our discussions so far. I know I've been feeling a little uncomfortable with the tensions, and some of the ground rules are not being followed."

EXERCISES IN PROCESS INTERVENTION

As a training exercise in facilitation workshops, participants are asked to consider the following scenarios and to answer three questions: 1) how they would intervene, 2) why they would choose that option, and 3) what they would do if their chosen intervention does not seem to be enough to restore collaboration or otherwise address the challenge. You might like to complete the same exercise and then review the discussion in Appendix G. In all cases, "you" refers to the facilitator.

1. When discussing proposed ground rules, one participant says, "I'm not agreeing to turn off my cell phone."

2. In the course of conversation, you notice that voices are rising, interruptions are becoming more frequent, and the meeting is becoming a shouting match.

3. You see that a lot of acronyms and jargon are being used and have reason to think that one or more of the participants are lost.

4. You notice that one participant is dominating the conversation and that all others tend to direct their comments and questions to her.

5. You notice that the parents tend to be very quiet; you sense that they are not happy but are just not speaking up and sharing what they think and feel.

6. The committee's chairperson has a very authoritative style, and others seem to be afraid to speak up and share.

7. The mother becomes tearful and others seem uncomfortable; the chairperson keeps the discussions going as if nothing were wrong.

8. A lot of time is spent repeating the same point at issue and the same demands and arguments; no progress is being made.

9. It seems clear that this meeting is not going to result in agreement.

10. You suspect that the proposed IEP is not compliant with federal law or district policy.

11. An agreement has been reached, but you have reason to believe that the plan is not workable and that the participants are just agreeing so they can be done and leave.

12. When you ask if any members have anything they might like to say before closing, you sense that some participants are upset but won't say anything.

6 Dealing with Impasse

In previous chapters, a number of scenarios were used to illustrate the issue of impasse and the options available to the facilitator when the team cannot seem to reach agreement. This chapter addresses this issue in more detail and reviews those interventions in an organized way. Because it is essential that a facilitator have the skills to manage impasse, and because those skills are sure to be required on many occasions, Appendix H summarizes these options for easy reference.

A helpful point of departure for the topic of impasse is to consider how to know when it has occurred.

Indicators of Impasse

The same issues are repeated without progress.

Team members are locked into opposing positions.

Comments are made, such as "This is a waste of time."

Threats are made, such as "I'll just have to file a complaint or request a due process hearing."

Members have nothing further to say.

One or more members have decided to end the meeting without agreement.

MOMENTARY IMPASSE

There are two forms of impasse: momentary and fatal. Momentary impasse occurs when a team has reached a standstill and yet agreement may still be possible during the meeting. This is in contrast to fatal impasse, in which it is clear that no agreement will be reached. One of the interesting features of this dichotomy is that "It ain't over till it's over," and one can never distinguish momentary from fatal until the group members decide to conclude their negotiations and/or one or more members actually walk out. In other words, every impasse must be assumed to be momentary until proven otherwise.

Because faith in the process is an essential element of collaboration, it is of critical importance that the facilitator never propose, support, or suggest failure. It could be very destructive to the team's potential for agreement if the facilitator were to say something like "It seems clear that you are not going to reach agreement about this." Instead, the facilitator must remain "the last man standing" when it comes to maintaining faith and trusting the process. This does not in any way imply that the team members are wrong to give up and quit, only that this decision must be squarely their own.

In their frustration due to their lack of skills, participants are very likely to give up long before they really need to, and if the facilitator can continue to maintain faith in the collaborative process and hold out possibilities for moving forward, this may make all the difference in terms of whether the meeting ends with an agreement. However, the facilitator must not become attached to the outcome of the meeting but only to supporting the collaborative process. That is, the facilitator must assist the team members to clearly see their issues and options so that they become empowered to make informed decisions, whatever they ultimately choose to do. This may seem like double-talk: The facilitator should not be attached to the outcome but should give the team every possible chance to come into agreement. And yet this may seem less contradictory when the emphasis is put not on the agreement but on the "every possible chance." *That* is the facilitator's role: to champion the cause of collaboration and provide all possible support for the collaborative process. Having done that, the facilitator can rest assured that the job has been done well and that any failure to reach consensus is *not* due to any failing on the part of the facilitator.

This last comment warrants some expansion. It cannot be assumed that just because a facilitator is present, the team will be greatly strengthened in its ability to resolve conflict and reach consensus. There is definitely such a thing as bad facilitation, which occurs when the facilitator either ignores important opportunities for intervention or intervenes in ways that are actually destructive. With this in mind, it is essential that a facilitator have a clear sense of what supports moving through impasse to consensus and what can hinder it or even accelerate failure.

OPTIONS FOR DEALING WITH IMPASSE

1. Reflect and Acknowledge

A facilitator can reflect and acknowledge the team's difficulty by saying, for example, "You all seem to be having a tough time right now." The purpose of reflecting and acknowledging is entirely a matter of recognition and empowerment. It allows the group members to step back from the content of their discussion (*what* they are discussing) and instead begin to look at their process (*how* they are discussing it) and how they might proceed more effectively. Here are some dos and don'ts:

Avoid: "You all are clearly at a standstill." [implying impossibility]

Avoid: "I don't see that this is going to be settled today." [reflecting in the negative]

Avoid: "You seem unable to move through this issue." [suggesting inability]

Consider: "This seems to be a challenging issue for you." [challenges can be overcome]

Consider: "I sense some frustrations and maybe some questions about how to get through this." [acknowledging feelings; using softening words such as "maybe" and "some"]

Consider: "Seems like some of you are feeling kind of discouraged." [acknowledging feelings; using softening words such as "seems like" and "kind of"]

2. Ask for Help; Invite Suggestions as to the Source of the Impasse

There are many possible sources of impasse (e.g., lack of information, different interpretations of behavior, hot tempers, unexpected information, hurt feelings, mistrust, different understandings of law and policies). Encouraging the group to identify its obstacles may open new doors for moving through them, as in asking, for example, "What do you think is making it hard for you to move through this issue?" Be alert that the team members may not directly answer the question, as in the following example:

Facilitator: This seems to be a hard issue for you. [reflecting for recognition]

Administrator: I don't see a resolution here.

Facilitator: *(to team)* What do you all think is making this so difficult today? [asking for help]

Parent: Well, Kevin is going to get that change in placement. There are no two ways about it. [note that the parent has not answered the question]

Facilitator: I can see that this is a very important issue for you. [reflecting for recognition] So what do you think is making it so hard for the team to come into agreement? [repeats question to raise awareness of the obstacles]

Parent: Well, I just don't think they are willing to consider any other ideas but their own.

Advocate: I think they're playing a little footloose with the law. Kevin has a right to an appropriate learning environment, and the one he is in is not appropriate.

Facilitator: Okay, so one obstacle may have to do with open minds and another might be recognition of legal rights. [repeating for recognition] Any other ideas?

Diagnostician: I think the data are revealing the needs, and the needs can still be addressed in his present placement.

Special education teacher: I think there are a lot of assumptions being made about how Kevin would do at that other campus.

Administrator: There's also the issue of district policy. We can't just move a student to a different campus if his educational needs can be met where he is currently placed.

Facilitator: Okay, so some see the difficulty with open minds, some with legal issues, some with unexplored options, some with policies and the authority of the team, some with assumptions that may or may not be correct. [repeating for recognition] So what might be your next steps? Any ideas about what could move you all forward? [asking for help]

Administrator: What if we meet again in a week or two and have someone from the district's central office here to participate in the discussion?

Special education teacher: I also think a site visit to the other campus would help clarify what services they do have and if there might be any downsides to such a move. I'd be willing to go with Mrs. Jones, if that would be okay with her.

Advocate: *(to parent)* I see some benefits to those suggestions. You don't have anything to lose. I think it could be worth a try.

And the team is collaborating once again. The key is to encourage the team members first to clarify what it is that is keeping them stuck and then to collaboratively and consensually make agreements about their disagreements. Examples of such agreements include the following:

- Deferring decision pending further information, such as additional testing or a site visit

- Deferring pending further thought and discussion—to take a break and come back with fresh minds and possibly new perspectives

- Deferring pending expert advice, such as from a behavior specialist, a legal expert, or a district-level administrator

- Seeking mediation

As long as the team members are making decisions together about how they wish to proceed, impasse has not yet occurred, and escalation into a due process hearing or a complaint investigation is much less likely. Incidentally, some people may take offense at any bias against these two forms of dispute resolution. Yet consider that both are very costly in terms of time and/or money, both lead to damaged relationships, and both are extremely adversarial, whereas the intention of the law is so clearly collaborative. Consider also how very unnecessary so many complaints and hearings may be. Why not reserve them for the few situations when they really are the best options and when other, less costly and less adversarial, approaches have been tried first?

3. Retrace the Day's Progress; Review What Has Been Agreed and What Remains Undecided

Helping the team to see how much it *has* achieved often restores faith in the collaborative process. This was illustrated in Chapter 3 with the following scenario, repeated here for purposes of review and organization:

Parent: If you're not going to get the one-to-one aide, then it's a waste of time to continue this meeting. I'm out of here.

Advocate: *(to parent)* I think it's obvious you're going to have to take this to a higher level.

Administrator: Mr. Washington, as much as I'd like to give you what you are asking for, I just don't feel that it's in your child's best interests.

Parent: If that's your position, then there's no point continuing this discussion. I'm out of here. [note that the group has reached an impasse]

Facilitator: *(sees that the team members have lost faith in their process and are focused only on their one point of disagreement after many points of agreement)* I sense some frustrations in the room. Would it make sense to maybe summarize what seems to have happened during this meeting? I've noticed a lot of progress made and quite a few points of agreement. [reflecting for recognition and asking permission to repeat for recognition]

Parent: Well, I don't see it, but go ahead.

(Other members nod in agreement.)

Facilitator: Well, please correct me if I'm wrong here. I think you all agreed that eligibility is still appropriate, right? And it sounds like everyone is seeing considerable progress in reading, am I right? And I noticed that you seemed in agreement that some follow-up testing would be a good thing prior to the next state testing, no? And I think you agreed that math continues to be very challenging for Mary and that additional help of some sort is going to be important. And you all seemed to share a concern with the question of timely exchange of information and proposed a plan whereby the teacher will call home and not just rely on Mary to share the message if it is something really important for the parents to receive. Am I right so far? *(Group nods in approval.)* Wow, sounds like you agreed on quite a lot today. So, then, the only point that seems really undecided is whether a teacher's aide is going to be the best way to give Mary the support in math class that you all agree is necessary. Am I wrong about that?

Parent: Well, she needs support, and I don't see why having an adult to work closely with her wouldn't be a simple solution to this problem. I think it's just the money. They don't want to spend the money.

Administrator: I'm not going to lie and say that the money isn't something we want to consider. I just assure you that it is not the deciding factor. I wouldn't recommend a teacher's aide for math support even if we had all the money in the world. It would just make her very dependent, and this could be very harmful for her in the long run.

Teacher: So what do you propose?

Administrator: Well, I'm not sure yet. How about we ask for a recommendation from the Education Service Center and meet again in, say, 2 weeks, to continue this discussion?

Parent: Okay, but I'm not sure I believe you.

Facilitator: So it sounds like you are agreed to have an expert make suggestions about how best to support Mary's math skills and then to meet again in 2 weeks to consider her recommendations, is that right?

(All nod in agreement.)

In the previous scenario, the team reached an impasse, retraced their progress, clarified their point of disagreement (the teacher's aide), and then made an agreement about their disagreement: to defer pending further information. In so doing, they have collaborated toward consensus and their impasse has been bridged.

4. Play with the Time Shape of a Proposal

Playing with the time shape of a proposal involves asking, for example, "What if you were to try it for, say, a month, and if it wasn't working, you could reassess and perhaps modify the plan? Does that idea have any value? What do you all think?" Playing with the time shape can often serve to break through an impasse because the group members may not come up with this idea on their own. The following scenario, which was based on a real-life situation, was introduced in Chapter 1 and discussed further in Chapter 5:

Speech therapist: I think your son would benefit from some time in the general classroom so he can model the speech of his peers.

Parent: Well, his doctor said he should have one-to-one therapy, so I don't want to agree to that.

Speech therapist: But there are things he will gain from his peers that just aren't the same one-to-one with an adult.

Parent: Well, I'm not going to agree to something that is not what his doctor recommended. [impasse has been reached]

Facilitator: So may I just check in and see if I'm understanding what you're saying? Would that be okay?

(Both nod.)

Facilitator: *(to parent)* Sounds like you're saying that the doctor made a recommendation and you don't want to go against that, is that right? [repeating for recognition]

Parent: Yes. That's right.

Facilitator: *(to speech therapist)* And you're saying that there are benefits that Andre would receive in the classroom that he can't get in one-to-one services with an adult, is that right?

Speech therapist: Right. They learn a lot from their peers.

Facilitator: Well, what would you think about maybe trying him in the general classroom for maybe a week or two and seeing how it goes? Then, if it doesn't seem to be a good idea, you could meet once again and reconsider. How does that sound? Any value in an idea like that? [playing with the time shape]

Parent: *(after a brief pause)* Okay. We can try it. But *(to speech therapist)* would you come with me to his next doctor's appointment so you can explain this to the doctor?

Speech therapist: Sure. I can do that.

By playing with the time shape, the team has made an agreement about their disagreement (to try it for a week or two); collaboration is restored and consensus has been reached.

5. Build in Guarantees and Contingencies ("If that happens, then. . .")

Very often, when people are at an impasse, it is because there is a fear or assumption that a certain negative event will or might occur if they agree to the particular proposal. Thus, a parent might be unwilling to agree to an individualized education program (IEP) because he believes the team will not follow through. A teacher might be unwilling to agree to a child remaining in his classroom because he believes the disruptive behaviors will be repeated. An administrator might be unwilling to agree to additional services because she believes she does not have the staff available to provide them. In all of these examples, there is an expectation of a negative consequence and the good intention of wanting to avoid it. As discussed in Chapters 3 and 5, whenever a person wants something, he or she is motivated by an "interest" that always involves an assumption of an anticipated benefit. Similarly, whenever a person *does not* want something, it is because of an interest in avoiding an anticipated harm. The problem, however, is that the issue may be reduced to an either/or, black/white, win/lose paradigm—either the IEP is signed or not, either the child stays in the classroom or not, either the service is provided or not. Very often, however, many more options—many shades of gray, in a sense—might come into clarity with continued collaboration.

One of the most helpful techniques for moving beyond the stone walls of impasse is to build in guarantees and contingencies. Playing with the time shape is similar in that it provides the guarantee that, if a certain thing were to happen (or not happen), the group will get back together to reassess and perhaps change the plan. But this intervention focuses only on the time frame of a proposal rather than on what exactly the team will do if the initial proposal fails. In other words, it does not specify the contingency plan other than that the team will meet again to create one.

Let's look now at some possible ways to build guarantees and contingencies into a team's decision-making process. The intervention is simple and twofold: identify the fear and then agree on a plan if the feared event should happen. Here are a few sample contingency plans that might be incorporated into an agreement in response to identified fears. Typically only one option would be adopted, but three are presented for each scenario just for purposes of illustration:

1. A parent is unwilling to agree to an IEP because he fears the team will not follow through. If the team does not follow through (the contingency), then the guarantee would be that:

    a. the parent can independently arrange for the agreed-upon services and the school will reimburse the expenses; or

    b.   the team will move the child to a different classroom where the parent feels more certain that the plan will be implemented; or

    c.   the team will provide a one-to-one aide for the remainder of the school year.

2.   A teacher is unwilling to agree to a child remaining in his classroom because she fears that his disruptive behaviors will be repeated. If that should happen, then

    a.   The child will be separated by a partition so that he will be unable to make physical contact with the other students in the classroom; or

    b.   A one-to-one aide will be provided for the remainder of the school year to closely monitor the child's behavior and be on hand to intervene; or

    c.   The child will be removed to the behavioral intervention class, and a manifestation determination review will be scheduled as required by law.

With regard to this last example and the term "manifestation determination review," the Individuals with Disabilities Education Improvement Act (IDEA) of 2004 (PL 108–446) states that: "within 10 school days of any decision to change the placement of a child with a disability because of a violation of a code of student conduct, the local educational agency, the parent, and relevant members of the IEP Team . . . shall review all relevant information . . . to determine—(I) if the conduct in question was caused by, or had a direct and substantial relationship to, the child's disability; or (II) if the conduct in question was the direct result of the local educational agency's failure to implement the IEP." ("Placement in Alternative Educational Setting," n.d., Paragraph E)

3.   An administrator is unwilling to agree to additional services because she fears to have insufficient staff to provide them. If there should not be staff available, then

    a.   The parent can independently arrange for an appropriately screened provider at his or her own expense; or

    b.   The team will coordinate with the Regional Center (a community agency serving those with disabilities) to provide the necessary staff; or

    c.   A parent volunteer will be assigned to provide the additional services.

An interesting feature of this process of building in guarantees is that, very often, the ones making the commitments see absolutely no likelihood that the contingency will ever have to be activated; for this reason they have no reservations about making the agreement! A simple illustration comes from divorce mediation. It is not uncommon for spouses to refuse to agree to an out-of-court settlement because they believe that the other spouse has all kinds of assets hidden away in secret accounts that have not been disclosed. The impasse arises because they fear losing their fair share if they settle, and they also fear renewing lengthy and costly legal proceedings if those hidden assets should some day be discovered. A contingency plan resolves the impasse: The parties enter into a mediated agreement that is signed by a judge and entered as an order of the court. Their agreement specifies that, in the event that undisclosed assets are discovered belonging to the husband, then all such assets shall immediately accrue to the wife. The wife breathes much easier, the husband feels just fine about the agreement because he knows there are no undisclosed assets, and the impasse has been bridged!

Returning to the IEP table, what words can the facilitator use to assist the team to consider a contingency plan? Well, the obvious first step is to simply ask the team for help, as in this scenario:

Parent: I'm not signing because you aren't going to do it anyway.

Facilitator: Sounds like there are some concerns about whether the IEP will be followed through, right? [reflecting for recognition]

Parent: Right.

Facilitator: Any ideas how you all might move forward with this concern? [asking for help]

Administrator: I don't see it—if the trust is so low.

Teacher: Not if those kinds of assumptions are going to be made.

Diagnostician: I think we're pretty well dead in the water.

Facilitator: Well, let's say for some reason the IEP *isn't* followed through. Is there anything that could be done about it? Any possibilities for what you might do if the worst case scenario were to happen? [asking for help and providing an opportunity for the team to consider a contingency/guarantee plan]

Parent: Yeah, they could fund a private school placement.

Administrator: Well, I don't see us doing that, and I feel very sure the IEP *will* be followed through.

Facilitator: Well, let's just say for some reason it isn't—just for instance. So if that were to happen, what might be done as a next step? [again, asking for help and consideration of a contingency plan]

Administrator: Well, one thing is that we could call another meeting at the earliest sign that it isn't being followed so we could address it right then and there. First of all, we have a legal obligation to implement the IEP, and second, I don't think anyone is going to sign an IEP they don't plan to carry out.

Facilitator: So how does that sound—that if anyone believes the IEP is not being followed, they request a meeting at the earliest possible opportunity so that any shortcomings can be addressed? [repeating for recognition and empowering by offering choice]

Parent: I agree so long as they put that in writing, but I want an interim meeting in a month just to see how things are going at that point.

Facilitator: Would that be acceptable to the team—an interim meeting in a month to see how things are going?

(All members agree, and the impasse has been bridged.)

6. Probe for the Benefits of Reaching Agreement Today (Shared Interests) and the Costs of Leaving without Agreement (Shared Risks)

In Chapter 3, it was emphasized that at every IEP meeting, the members will have certain shared interests and certain shared risks. Shared interests include ensuring the progress and well-being of the student, making good use of time, having positive team spirit, having a sense of accomplishment, being heard, being understood, and so forth. Shared risks include escalating tensions, wasted time, damaged team relationships, the costs of legal representation, and a possible due process hearing or complaint investigation. It was also mentioned that a universal principle at work in negotiation is that *avoiding a shared risk is always a shared interest.* A facilitator can use this principle to help the team members move through their impasse by asking them to consider (recognize) the advantages and disadvantages of ending the meeting without an agreement. We can use an impasse scenario presented earlier in this chapter to illustrate this intervention approach:

Parent: If you're not going to get the one-to-one aide, then it's a waste of time to continue this meeting. I'm out of here.

Advocate: *(to parent)* I think it's obvious you're going to have to take this to a higher level.

Administrator: Mr. Washington, as much as I'd like to give you what you are asking for, I just don't feel that it's in your child's best interests.

Parent: I'm out of here.

Facilitator: *(sees that the meeting is about to end in failure to reach an agreement and in a loss of collaboration)* Mr. Washington, I hear you saying that this is a waste of time and you're out of here, is that right? [repeating for recognition]

Parent: Right.

Facilitator: [shifts from a transformative to facilitative approach because it seems clear that the team is unlikely to resolve this on its own] Is everyone in agreement that terminating the meeting now would be your best next step? Does anyone see any downsides to leaving at this point? [probing for interests—what the team members see as their shared risks]

Administrator: Well, I think we could work this out if Mr. Washington would just work with us.

Facilitator: So you think there is still hope to work this out? [repeating for recognition]

Administrator: Yes, I do.

Facilitator: *(seeing that the question of downsides was not answered)* Does anyone see any downsides if you did just end the meeting at this point? [probing for interests]

Special education teacher: Well, I think Mr. Washington is talking about a due process hearing or complaint with the state, and I think that would be very unfortunate.

Facilitator: Very unfortunate. [repeating for recognition]

Special education teacher: Well, yes. It would take so much time and lead to so much bad feeling. It's just not necessary.

Facilitator: So you see some downsides in the time involved and the damage to your team relationships, is that right? *(Special education teacher nods in agreement.)* So does everyone agree that this might lead to lots of time spent and lots of bad feelings? *(All agree; parent seems to be stopping to consider.)* So, it sounds like you are all in agreement about the downsides of wasted time and damaged relationships, am I right? [reflecting their common interest in avoiding two shared risks] *(All nod in agreement.)* So does anyone see any options? [asking for help]

Administrator: *(to parent)* Mr. Washington, I hope you will continue to explore options with us and see if we can't work this out.

Teacher: I'd like you to give us a chance.

Advocate: *(to parent)* You can always file later if you want to.

Parent: Okay. So what else could you do for my daughter, if you won't get her an aide?

And the team is collaborating once again.

FATAL IMPASSE

Let's assume that many or even all of the foregoing options have been tried, but to no avail. It is clear that the meeting is about to end without an agreement. What then can be done? Here are some possibilities:

7. Propose Another Meeting, Perhaps with a Different Facilitator

Although not clearly documented, it has been said that a second mediation has the same high probability of success as the first. If this is true, then it stands to reason that a second facilitation would also have a high probability of success. Although quantifiable success rates for facilitated IEP meetings are hard to find, a figure of 75% or more is starting to emerge with some consistency: Michigan, 83% ("IEP/IFSP Facilitation—Michigan," n.d.); Minnesota, 91% ("Facilitated IEP/IFSP/IIIP—Minnesota," n.d.); North Carolina, 73% for complete consensus and 95% for partial consensus ("Facilitated IEP Meetings—North Carolina," n.d.); Pennsylvania, 86% (Rider & Smith, n.d.; PowerPoint file "Dixie Rider Session 3.2—Presentation," slide 51). If a second facilitation has the same probability of success as the first, it might be well worth considering, and yet this option may not be something that the team members will think of on their own.

Those who fail to reach agreement at mediation or facilitation the first time around may assume that a second attempt would do them no good. As a champion for collaboration, however, the facilitator can encourage the team members to consider the possibility of continuing their discussions, perhaps with a different facilitator. Regardless of whether the facilitator sees himself or herself in any way responsible for the inability of the team to reach consensus, it costs nothing and does no harm to hold out hope that, perhaps with a different facilitator, the team might make greater progress. The facilitator's words might be something to the effect of "They say that a second meeting has the same high probability of success as the first. What would you think about the possibility of meeting again, possibly with a different facilitator, to see if that might help you all reach an agreement? Any possible value in that idea?" If the team members say no, at least the possibility has been raised for their consideration (recognition) and they have been given the choice (empowerment) as to how they wish to proceed.

8. Propose Mediation

Most states reporting on the success of their mediation programs in special education report a 75% to 85% settlement rate, with some notable exceptions, both higher and lower. This information can be found in Part B of the standardized Annual Performance Reports submitted by all states to the federal government. Aspects of these reports are summarized by the Center for Appropriate Dispute Resolution in Special Education, usually known as CADRE (http://www.directionservice.org/cadre; for settlement rates, compare

Table 6.1. Statistics from The Data Accountability Center for the year 2007–2008: Requests for mediations, due process hearings, and complaint investigations

	Total Requests 2007–2008		
	Mediations	Due process	Complaint investigations
Alabama	78	99	29
California	2,624	2,398	1,034
D.C.	11	3,261	7
Iowa	32	6	6
Kentucky	27	18	19
Maryland	318	324	86
North Carolina	105	56	115
South Dakota	5	2	19
Texas	302	300	425
Vermont	30	23	21
Wisconsin	94	37	104

From The Data Accountability Center (https://www.ideadata.org/PartBDispRes.asp)

Mediations Agreements Total to Mediations Held Total by year, "Summary of National Dispute Resolution Data," n.d.).

Of course, one can never predict what will happen in any individual case, and yet in general, mediation has a very high success rate and a very high satisfaction rate among those who are willing to use it. The problem, however, is that mediation is very much underutilized in just about every state that offers it (and all do, because it has been a requirement under federal law since the reauthorization of IDEA in 1997 [PL 105-17]). One can clearly see that it is an underutilized service by simply comparing the numbers of due process hearings and complaint investigations requested in almost any state relative to the numbers of mediations requested. Consider the statistics available from The Data Accountability Center for the year 2007–2008 for a sampling of 10 states and the District of Columbia (see Table 6.1). Very few states show a higher number of mediations requested relative to the combined total of due process hearing and complaint investigation requests. The few states that do (such as Iowa) may have valuable lessons to offer to others.

This underutilization is unfortunate from a number of perspectives, including the unnecessary costs, lost time, damaged relationships, and relinquishing by the parties of their decision-making authority. But it is also important to consider that, since the reauthorization of IDEA in 1997, federal law has clearly encouraged the use of mediation instead of—or at least prior to—the use of more adversarial approaches: "Thus, changes in the law, including provisions that require that mediation be available to parents, were designed to save money and reduce discord by encouraging parents and educators to work out their differences using non-adversarial means" (Abt Associates, 2002, p. 32). This encouragement was taken a step further with the December 2004 reauthorization of IDEA requiring that mediation services be provided for *any* matter in dispute in special education, whether or not a due process hearing had been requested. Note that

> IDEA 2004: 1. Requires that mediation is available whether or not there is a request for a due process hearing. Any state education agency (SEA) or local education agency (LEA) that receives assistance under Part B shall ensure that procedures are established and implemented to allow parties to disputes involving any matter, including matters arising prior to the filing of a due process hearing request pursuant to Section 615(b)(6), to resolve such disputes through a mediation process. [615(e)(1)] (http://www.eed.state.ak.us/tls/sped/pdf/OSEP/tb-safeguards-2.pdf)

Prior to this change, state-provided mediation was usually more closely tied to due process hearings.

Given its high rates of success and satisfaction, one may wonder why mediation is not being used much more often. After all, it is the only one of the three legally prescribed options (the others being hearings and complaints) in which the parties retain their roles as decision makers. In contrast, in a hearing or complaint, a hearing officer or the state department of education makes the final decisions *for* the parties. Mediation is also the only one of the three options that has the potential for a win/win outcome, because the parties may freely accept or reject whatever settlement offers are being made, which is not the case when decisions are made by a hearing officer or the department of education. Why then is mediation not more widely used? The answer probably has much to do with the education of the consumer (school personnel, parents, lawyers, and advocates) and with a cultural mindset that seems more willing to meet on the field of battle than at the conference table. In this respect, the facilitator can help.

Again, as a champion for the process of collaboration, the facilitator might share with the parties that "One option at this point might be to consider mediation. States report very high success and satisfaction rates, and you really would have nothing to lose because you wouldn't have to accept anything that didn't feel acceptable to you. You could also still consider a complaint investigation or due process hearing if you wanted to—you wouldn't be closing doors to those options. Does mediation sound like something worth a try? Anyone see any possible benefits if you were to go that route?" Obviously, this is a far more informative style than a facilitator would normally use, but it is certainly permissible within the facilitative model, which allows participation in option generation that supports the process of collaboration. Mediation, with all its advantages, may not be an option the parties would recognize, understand, or consider on their own.

9. Narrow the Issues in Dispute by Summarizing the Agreements Made (Perhaps in Writing) and Highlighting the Points Left Undecided

Experience has shown that parties in negotiation are often all too willing to throw the baby out with the bath water by leaving *everything* undecided just because *some* things are undecided. Thus, a team might be discussing, say, seven issues at a meeting, and most of them may be agreed upon, leaving only one or two to be settled by some other method. Why then put everything back into dispute?

In an earlier section of this chapter, under "Retrace the Day's Progress," the following example of narrowing the issues was provided:

Facilitator: Well, please correct me if I'm wrong here. I think you all agreed that eligibility is still appropriate, right? And it sounds like everyone is seeing considerable progress in reading, am I right? And I noticed that you seemed in agreement that some follow-up testing would be a good thing prior to the next state testing, no? And I think you agreed that math continues to be very challenging for Mary and that additional help of some sort is going to be important. And you all seemed to share a concern with the question of timely exchange of information and proposed a plan whereby the teacher will call home and not just rely on Mary to share the message if it is something really important for the parents to receive. Am I right so far? *(Group nods in approval.)* Wow, sounds like you agreed on quite a lot today. So, then, the only point that seems really undecided is whether a teacher's aide is going to be the best way to give Mary the support in math class that you all agree is necessary. Am I wrong about that?

If this scenario were reduced to a list form of agreements and disagreements, it would look like this:

Agreed	Undecided
Child is still eligible for special education	One-to-one aide
Reading progress has been considerable	
Follow-up testing is needed	
Math remains a challenge	
Math support is needed	
Timely exchange of information is required	
A plan for information has been made	

Given the many points of agreement, why not narrow the issues in dispute by documenting the agreements in some written form and placing only the one undecided issue before a hearing officer or the department of education? Think of the time and money that could be saved by doing so, as well as how much decision-making authority could then remain with the team members and all that they *have* achieved through collaboration. As another benefit, the team could implement their agreed-upon points right away without any need to wait for the results of a hearing or complaint investigation.

Narrowing the issues in dispute is another idea that team members may not think of on their own. More than once, as a divorce mediator, I have seen parties take a tentative settlement agreement to their lawyers for review, and an attorney has had concerns about one or another point among the parties' many points of agreement. But never once have I seen an attorney recommend that the parties return to mediation to iron out the details in question. Instead, the entire agreement was discarded and *all* of the issues were then put before the court, obligating both sides to incur extensive legal expenses and divesting them of all authority as decision makers in their own futures.

Returning to the facilitation of IEP meetings, what then could the facilitator do to assist in narrowing the issues in dispute? Well, he or she could use words to the effect of "It seems that you have quite a few points of agreement as a result of your discussions today—eligibility, progress, testing, need for math support, and a plan for more timely exchange of information. The one point that remains without agreement has to do with the one-to-one aide. It also sounds like you are very sure that you want to take that issue to a higher authority. So might it be helpful in any way to narrow the issues you take to the hearing officer or department of education—for example, summarizing in writing what is agreed and leaving the authorities to decide that one remaining point of disagreement? Does anyone see any value in that idea?" Without the facilitator to call this collaborative option to the attention of the team, the members might never recognize that they have such a choice and thus would not be empowered to act on it.

10. Invite Agreements About the Disagreements— How Do the Team Members Wish to Proceed?

In the end, if at all possible, the impasse can still be collaborative if the members can agree on how they wish to proceed from this point forward. Can they perhaps agree that a due process hearing *is* the best next step for them? Can they perhaps agree that consulting with lawyers and then making their decision is the step they now wish to take? Regardless of what the team members are considering, either together or individually, any agreements they are able to make may serve to keep the ball in the collaborative court while minimizing the damage to their future working relationship and perhaps even opening doors toward consensus in the future. Thus, for example, perhaps the meeting will end without agreement on an IEP but *with* agreement that the members will consult with their lawyers in preparation for whatever they wish to do next. Suppose this is done with smiles and handshakes and yet another agreement: to touch base after talking with the lawyers to see what new ideas or possibilities may have come to light by that time. Isn't it possible that, by then, the team may have gathered new information that might prove helpful in creating new proposals and reaching consensus after all? If nothing else, the doors to communication will remain open and the process of recognition and empowerment will continue for the benefit of all involved.

7 Establishing IEP Facilitation

Facilitation offers so many advantages that it is no surprise that, in a very real sense, it is sweeping the nation as more and more states are making it available. At this time, it is not legislated in any way, and so it is entirely optional. But if a state, school district, or other agency wanted to develop the capacity for facilitated individualized education program (IEP) meetings, what could it do? That is the subject of this chapter.

WHO WILL FACILITATE?

One of the first questions to be considered is who will serve as facilitators, and this question has several facets. Will the facilitators be school personnel, community professionals, community volunteers, or parent–school co-facilitators? How will they be trained or otherwise qualified? What philosophical model will they represent, and how will they define their roles? What accountability will they have?

The realm of facilitation is very much an emerging practice, and programs in many states have been developed only within the past few years. It is thus difficult to speak in more than general terms because the picture is constantly changing. With that said, one of the most helpful resources is the Center for Appropriate Dispute Resolution in Special Education (CADRE), funded by the Office of Special Education Programs of the U.S. Department of Education. Among its responsibilities are to serve as a central clearinghouse for information and to sponsor periodic conferences that invite representatives from all states and territories to share experiences and, in a sense, form a learning community of interested parties. In October 2005, CADRE sponsored a national conference on the facilitation of IEP meetings, the first of its kind, and material from the conference sessions is available online (see "CADRE's National Symposium on IEP Facilitation," n.d.). Another invaluable and evolving resource developed by CADRE is a brief comparative summary of facilitation programs and contact people in at least 18 states (see "Process and Practice Information," n.d.). Unless otherwise noted, the details in this section are taken from that source.

IEP facilitators may come from many walks of life. In some states, such as Wisconsin, professional mediators are contracted from the general community. Indiana uses a co-facilitation model, turning to a parent advocate and school professional facilitating together. New Hampshire uses volunteers who have received special training from the state department of education. Similarly, Maryland uses community volunteer mediators who have received additional specialized training. North Dakota relies on professors from the special education programs of its state universities. Delaware's facilitators are provided through a program of the University of Delaware. Iowa facilitators "may be either an individual from within the school district who is considered neutral to the conflict or an individual selected from outside the district in which the conflict has occurred" ("Process and Practice Information," n.d.). New Mexico has two facilitation programs. One provides facilitation of formal complaints by means of a Complaint Assistance IEP, which "is an IEP meeting that is facilitated by the representative of the public agency who directs special education programs within the public agency, and who has decision-making authority on behalf of such agency" ("Process and Practice Information," n.d.). The other is conducted by New Mexico's special education mediators and relates to IEP meetings that do not involve a formal complaint. Texas is in the earliest stages of developing facilitation of IEP meetings and is primarily training school personnel to serve as facilitators within their own or nearby districts, however the option is open for districts to employ independent facilitators from the general community if they prefer.

Let's consider some of the advantages and disadvantages of the different facilitator pools. These include such variables as training and experience; philosophy and roles; availability, costs, and logistics; content knowledge and bias; and accountability.

Training and Experience

The training of facilitators really has only one practical purpose, which is to produce *qualified* facilitators. Because facilitators can come from many walks of life, the training they require may vary in quantity and in scope. For example, if the facilitators are professors of special education, they will require little or no training in special education terminology or the IEP environment, and the training they require may have to be more focused on collaborative decision making and on methods of facilitation. In contrast, community mediators may have considerable experience in facilitation but little or no knowledge of the school and IEP environments or their terminology, administration, and responsibilities; they may also require training in team facilitation and how it may differ from two-party dispute resolution.

The training I have developed and implemented has been designed primarily for school professionals. It is a 12-hour experiential workshop titled "Advanced Facilitation in the IEP Environment." A recommended prerequisite is completion of another 12-hour workshop, "Collaboration in the IEP Environment." This prerequisite training is for any school professional who participates in IEP meetings and is especially intended for those who chair the meetings. Topics include common sources of parent dissatisfaction and recommendations for prevention; effective meeting management; collaboration and consensus; principled negotiation; communication pitfalls and alternatives; the emotional side of living; keys to diplomacy; conflict indicators at the local, state, and national levels; conflict resolution interventions; and follow-up activities. Most of these topics are considered essential background for facilitators based on the very simple notion that a facilitator benefits from understanding what makes for effective collaborative meetings before he or she can master the skills necessary for restoring collaboration when it is lost. In contrast, the training in facilitation skills focuses on a different role—not of chairperson or team member but rather of the outside neutral who is not a decision maker or an advisor but who can support the team to communicate effectively and arrive at its own consensus-based decisions.

The content of that facilitation training has been adapted into a textbook format here, a principal difference being the opportunity for participant sharing through structured exercises and extensive role plays. The 12-hour, 2-day workshop format was chosen based on the difficulties associated with taking school personnel away from their other responsibilities to attend training events; time is precious and more than 2 days is just not workable for most of the people who would like to attend. It is also based on the fact that those attending will already be certified professionals with considerable experience in the IEP environment and will have completed the 12-hour prerequisite training in collaboration and conflict resolution, or equivalents. "Equivalents" might include other, comparable professional training or study of the textbook based on that training, *A Guide to Collaboration for IEP Teams* (Martin, 2005). Finally, it must be emphasized that new learning is a "highly perishable commodity," and periodic follow-up is essential for review, for solidification of gains, and for continued progress once the participants begin to have field experience in facilitation. Such follow-up is provided in 4- to 6-hour modules, and it is recommended that practicing facilitators participate at least twice a year. In all, then, this training amounts to 24 hours (or equivalents) plus follow-up and is intended for those who are already well familiar with the IEP environment.

The training that will be most appropriate for any given state or agency will depend on many factors, some of which may be very different than those just described. As one example, the Dispute Resolution Association of Michigan trains all of its mediators in IEP facilitation through a separate IEP facilitation training module. They must complete 40 hours of training; fulfill a 10-hour internship; mediate at least 25 hours of non–special education disputes; complete 16 hours of advanced mediation training in special education matters; and attend a day-long update training on mediation/facilitation training skills and special education issues at least once every 2 years ("IEP/IFSP Facilitation—Michigan," n.d.).

As another example, Maryland uses volunteers from community mediation centers and describes their training as follows: "The facilitator has completed a 50-hour training course in mediation skills, has experience mediating a variety of disputes, and has completed a 3-day training in IEP Facilitation" (Maryland State Department of Education, 2007, p. 1). Details on training programs used in other states may be found by contacting the "practice authors" on CADRE's web site ("Process and Practice Information," n.d.).

Philosophy and Roles of the Facilitator

Although facilitation is still in the formative stages, certain consistencies are beginning to emerge among states. The initial statistical data, despite being limited in quantity and subject to a great many variables, all point in the same direction: Facilitation of IEP meetings has very high success rates and very high satisfaction rates. As mentioned in Chapter 6, figures of 73% to 95% have been reported to CADRE. Another commonality has to do with the philosophy and role of the facilitator, with some states clearly specifying that their facilitators will not offer advice or recommendations but instead only support the process of the team as the members develop the content of their own decisions.

In terms of the best sources for IEP facilitators, with appropriate training any of the sources described in the summaries provided to CADRE can be very effective ("Process and Practice Information," n.d.). Thus, any of them can be recommended, provided that the focus is on supporting the team's collaborative process as opposed to advising or directing with regard to content. In other words, the critical variable is not *who* the facilitators are but what they do, meaning how they support the process of the IEP team.

After initial experience with directive facilitation, Pennsylvania recognized the limitations of that approach and shifted to a facilitative model (Rider & Smith, n.d.; see especially the PowerPoint file "Dixie Rider Session 3.2—Presentation," slides 9-11). On the basis of lessons learned, Pennsylvania developed the following recommendations (slide 27):

- Facilitative method only

- Not a member of the team

- IEP team owns the IEP

- LEA [local education agency; i.e., school district or charter school] runs the meeting

- Facilitator's role is only to enhance communication and to help sides address disagreements or conflict relating to IEP only

- Facilitator offers no technical assistance or input regarding content

- Facilitator sits in silence if parties are moving forward

This Pennsylvania summary is entirely consistent with the philosophy of facilitation presented in this book with the exception (here) of an emphasis on transformative approaches first and facilitative methods when the team requires the additional support. This may, however, just be a matter of semantics: The term *facilitative* is frequently used in discussions of IEP facilitation but is rarely defined in more than general terms.

Availability, Costs, and Logistics

The logistics of facilitation present some interesting challenges and may have a bearing on the decisions made, whether at the state or district level. Some of these challenges have to do with the coordination of the program, which is a topic we will return to in a moment. In terms of who will serve as facilitators, there are a number of logistical issues to be considered. One has to do with costs.

In most larger, urban areas, mediation is readily available, and one can look in the yellow pages or phone the local courthouses for details. Many larger communities have court-connected mediation programs for one or more of the following: juvenile offenders, adult offenders, small claims court, community disputes, municipal court, domestic relations, and general civil litigation. These programs are often staffed by volunteers, and little or no costs are associated for participants. Provided that the mediation is facilitative or transformative in design, these programs may offer a ready pool of trained and experienced mediators who could easily transition into the role of IEP facilitators with supplementary training, as is done in several states, as mentioned earlier. The phrase "provided that the mediation is facilitative or transformative" warrants some expansion.

Many volunteer mediation programs *require* that their mediators use facilitative or transformative approaches, but this is not necessarily true, especially in court-related matters where the mediators may be attorneys. The attorney mediators are often selected precisely because of their content knowledge and ability to forecast likely outcomes at trial and make recommendations for settlement based on their legal experience. The use of such directive approaches is hotly debated within the mediation community, and many practitioners question whether directive/evaluative mediation should even be called mediation at all, as opposed to "early neutral evaluation" or "settlement conference." That evaluative methods will be used is not *inherently* the case when attorneys serve as mediators; the real issue is the philosophy they espouse and the training they may have received in facilitative or transformative methods. In contrast, non-attorney mediators tend to more comfortably adopt a facilitative or transformative style. The point, for present purposes, is that it is not enough to simply turn to the court- or community-based mediation programs for appropriate facilitators; the question of the training and philosophical orientation of those mediators will also be an important one to ask.

Another option as a source for facilitators is to look in the yellow pages for professional mediators in private practice. Some states employ such people on a contract basis, maintaining a roster of approved and qualified professionals who can be called upon as needed in response to requests for IEP facilitation. Of course, the costs may vary. Minnesota reports an average of $924 per facilitation, attributable in part to the fact that 46% of facilitations require more than one meeting ("Facilitated IEP/IFSP/IIIP—Minnesota," n.d.). North Dakota, which uses special education professors, cites costs of $75 per hour for preparation time and actual facilitation, $50 per hour for travel time, plus travel expenses, adding that "the average time spent for our facilitators in prep-time is 4.5 hours. The average time spent in actual facilitation for our facilitators is 3 hours" ("IEP Facilitation—North Dakota," n.d.). This calculates to an average cost per facilitation of roughly $560 plus travel time and expenses.

Of course, the issue of funding a facilitation program is a huge consideration in itself. This funding is not just related to the compensation of the facilitators but also to the administration of programs and the associated costs of web sites and advertising. Obviously, these costs will depend on many factors, one of the first being, again, *who* will serve as facilitators. Another is the number of facilitations being provided, which will depend on the population and the amount of advertising to potential consumers of the service. This number is sure to increase dramatically with the passage of time, as facilitation gains more and more familiarity and acceptance among those who may choose to use it. A final consideration with regard to funding is distance. It is surely a safe assumption that the travel-related logistics of providing facilitators will differ enormously in Rhode Island and Delaware as compared with Texas or Alaska.

States that consider using school professionals to serve as facilitators face another set of challenges. Given how very busy nearly all school professionals are, how easily can they be freed from their other responsibilities to facilitate multi-hour or multi-session IEP meetings? How flexibly can they adjust their schedules to accommodate requests that may be made on short notice? How easily can they be released to attend continuing education in the form of follow-up training sessions?

One of the considerations that led Texas to choose to use school professionals as facilitators, at least initially, had to do with the expectation of reduced costs, given that school personnel are already salaried employees and would presumably charge nothing for their time to facilitate. Another factor was the school professionals' familiarity with the IEP process, the responsibilities of the team, and the terminology. Another consideration was travel: If districts supply their own facilitators (rather than have them provided from a statewide pool), these people are presumably local, and thus travel time and expenses will be minor concerns. It also seemed safe to assume that, if given a choice between a school professional or an outside neutral, parents would probably prefer an outside neutral, even if high costs were involved, because any school professional would presumably be biased. The next section examines these issues of knowledge of the IEP environment and of possible bias in more detail.

The Issue of Content Knowledge

A question that is often discussed (and even hotly debated) among mediators, and is equally relevant among facilitators, is how much "content knowledge" is needed to be an effective support to the team. *Content knowledge* refers to familiarity with the topics being discussed (in this case, at the IEP meeting) and includes such things as the purpose of the IEP team; the format of meetings; the team's obligations and constraints; relevant laws and policies; professional terminology, jargon, and acronyms; testing details and results; school administration and the roles of the team members; knowledge of the particular student and the current IEP; educational resources and options for meeting the student's individual needs; and the history of the team and its disagreements. How much of this does a skilled facilitator need to know? The answer depends entirely on the role the facilitator will play. If he or she will be directive and/ or informative, obviously the more content knowledge the better. But if the facilitator will remain true to the facilitative and transformative models, then content knowledge is essential *for the team members* but of very little relevance to the facilitator. In contrast, the facilitator's required knowledge is in the realm of *process* expertise, because a thorough understanding of how to build, support, and restore collaboration will be the lion's share of the work. Can the facilitator then have *no* content knowledge? This seemingly complex issue becomes very simple when we return to the facilitator's job description: The facilitator needs only as much content knowledge as is necessary to support the collaborative process of the team.

In this regard, it is important that the facilitator understand the purpose and responsibilities of the IEP team. Being familiar enough with the terminology to keep up with the discussions is helpful but not essential, because if the facilitator is lost, there is a good chance that others are lost as well. In short, having a thumbnail familiarity with the IEP environment is all that is necessary to facilitate (as opposed to direct) the meeting.

Every environment has its job-specific language, acronyms, and jargon. The perspective suggested here—that thumbnail familiarity is sufficient— is supported by my experience in U.S. Postal Service mediation, court-connected mediation, and business mediation and facilitation. As long as *the participants* understand their language, the facilitator can support their process; if, for any reason, they do not, the facilitator can then make it grist for the mill and assist the team members to communicate more effectively by using terms they can all understand. When it comes to content knowledge, it thus makes perfect sense that states are encountering high success rates by providing some limited supplementary training for those coming in as mediators from other areas of endeavor (e.g., Michigan, New Hampshire, and Maryland, as mentioned previously).

Before leaving this issue of content knowledge, it must be emphasized that this topic is not as simple or as settled as it may appear, nor is there universal agreement among facilitators. As mentioned in Chapter 5, some states and agencies have taken a specific stance on the subject, saying that their facilitators will not participate in giving information or in generating options but will, instead, leave the content of the IEP discussions entirely up to the committee members. However, not all states, agencies, or facilitators have a clear policy in this regard. Perhaps the bigger issue is not what content knowledge the facilitator may or may not have but how the facilitator will use such knowledge and what expectations the IEP team members will have of him or her. Thus, an appropriate first step for any facilitator will be to determine whether a governing state or agency policy is in place. Also, providing clarity to the team members prior to or at the start of the meeting will help to ensure that all participants have similar expectations. This can be done through the routine telephone contacts with parents and chairperson described in Chapter 4, opening remarks when the team assembles, and printed information and agreement forms, such as those appearing in Appendixes J and K.

What About Bias?

What about the issue of bias? This is especially relevant when school professionals serve as facilitators of IEP meetings. The question can easily arise: How can they possibly be neutral? When it comes to bias, two issues are important to consider. One is the existence of true bias, which occurs when the neutral really is allied with one side or another. The other has to do with the *perception* of bias when none exists at all. Both can be fatal to the ability of the facilitator to support the collaborative process of the team, and yet both can be effectively addressed.

Every facilitator must clearly understand how detrimental to the role of the neutral any true bias would be. Simply stated, if the neutral cannot adopt an impartial stance, regardless of the content of the discussion, then he or she would do well to recuse himself or herself and not take the case. Such bias might occur when the facilitator has personal knowledge of the student or the participants or has strong opinions about the issues in dispute. Another appropriate time to decline the role of facilitator would be when the facilitator believes that remaining impartial would be difficult. One example might be when his or her own colleagues or supervisors are expecting the facilitation to ensure a certain outcome, in which case the facilitator might feel pressured into a hidden agenda of his or her own (i.e., to satisfy those expectations).

A common concern of school professionals in facilitation training is "How can I be an administrator they can come to for guidance one day and just be a wishy-washy 'What do you all think?' kind of person the next?" or "How can I be the diagnostician they can come to for information one day but now refuse to answer when the team asks me specific questions?" The answers to such questions depend on a clear understanding of the role of the facilitator and on an ability to "switch hats" as required when in the facilitator's chair. What will also have a great bearing on this issue are the pre-meeting telephone conferences with the parent and chairperson, discussed in Chapter 4. That is the time when the facilitator will explain his or her role and assure the parties that, even though he or she is employed by the district, he or she intends to be impartial to any side or position and will only be there to help the team members develop a plan that they can all feel good about. "Making a deal" by asking the team members to point out if at any time they perceive the facilitator to be biased also helps allay concerns while providing an avenue for intervention should the issue arise. This can be done both on the phone before the meeting and in the introductory remarks at the start of the meeting. Given the difficulty of switching hats, one solution might be for school professionals to facilitate for other schools or nearby districts rather than the ones in which they serve in their administrative or professional roles.

In short, bias is not inherently involved when school professionals serve as facilitators. However, the perception and assumption of bias are very likely to arise, at least initially, and the facilitator should be prepared to address them both proactively, in terms of prevention, and again if any concerns should in fact be raised by the team. If handled this way, the appearance of bias should be meaningfully put to rest. In all probability, the fear of bias will usually be much bigger than the reality of it.

Accountability

Most states that use facilitation help to ensure quality by making data collection and participant surveys inherent parts of their facilitation programs. Some states post their facilitation-related materials online, including facilitation evaluation forms (see, e.g., North Carolina, http://www.ncpublicschools.org/ec/policy/dispute/meeting; Wisconsin, http://www.wsems.us/pdf/07.08_IEP_Participant_survey.pdf). It is highly recommended that a process for gathering feedback and collecting data be incorporated into any facilitation program. A helpful summary of topics to include can be found in "Twenty Questions You Should Answer Before Creating an IEP Meeting Facilitation System," developed by Kathy Wian of the University of Delaware and available online (Wian, n.d.). The relevant section on evaluation is presented here, and the entire document appears with permission as Appendix I:

6. How will the system be evaluated and what information will be tracked?

    a. Number of cases?
    b. Number of meetings?
    c. Hours spent per meeting or per case?
    d. Issues discussed?
    e. School, district, or county using the service?
    f. Outcome of each meeting?
    g. Whether the team reached consensus on the IEP?
    h. Satisfaction level of all meeting participants?
    i. Facilitator's performance?
    j. Other indicators for success?
    k. Follow-up after the case?
    l. Is this system tracked in conjunction w/other resolution systems?

An additional essential element of accountability is the ongoing training of facilitators through continuing education. As mentioned previously, Michigan requires such participation at least once every 2 years, and I recommend it perhaps twice a year at least for beginning facilitators.

Finally, it is recommended that facilitators be subject to periodic observation by those who provide training in this area. This is an option in the U.S. Postal Service program for the mediation of discrimination complaints. The purpose of such observation is to ensure that prescribed approaches are being used and to provide continuing education through feedback to the mediators. Being observed actually facilitating an IEP meeting can offer considerable benefits not easily provided in any other way.

WHO WILL COORDINATE?

From a review of the summaries posted through CADRE, it seems clear that most states centralize their facilitation programs by coordinating them through the state department of education. Thus, in many states one can find information about facilitation and even schedule it through a designated department at the state level. There are many advantages to centralizing facilitation services in this way. These include standardization of procedures, consistency of information, and public education through brochures and web sites dedicated to the facilitation of special education meetings. Another advantage is that it removes any link to the school district with which a person might have a dispute or a history of mistrust. This reduces the likelihood that bias will occur or be perceived. Also, those serving at the state level are more likely to be closely connected to continuing education, research, and recommended practices, especially if supporting the state's facilitation program is their only responsibility. Yet another consideration is the broader view of what is happening within the state and the state's ability to coordinate resources in a logistical sense—by knowing which facilitators are located where, what their availability is, and where they stand in terms of having fulfilled continuing education requirements. Such a statewide department can also serve as a resource for recruiting and training facilitators while also responding to any concerns that might arise with regard to the facilitators' professionalism, ethics, and adherence to appropriate styles of practice.

Another benefit of coordination at the statewide level is that consumers (i.e., parents, school personnel, advocates, and attorneys) are already familiar with turning to such a central resource, much as they have been doing for years for other dispute-related services. In addition, the state may be in the ideal position to gather data and feedback on the effectiveness of a facilitation program and to make course corrections as necessary for improvement as experience is gained and lessons are learned.

But what if a particular state does not yet have a facilitation program? Is it necessary to wait until it develops one? Well, any school district could establish a facilitation program at the local level, but most of the same requirements would have to be in place as those described above—coordinating a pool of facilitators, informing the consumer, providing support and training, standardizing procedures, and serving as a resource for questions and concerns. Facilitation could also be provided by non-school agencies, such as parent or advocacy groups, universities, mediation services, private consultants, or agencies providing services to people with disabilities. However, because they are outside the educational hierarchy, such agencies are likely to face a significant marketing challenge in terms of persuading school districts or individual schools to use their services (although it certainly can and has been done).

WHO WILL TELL THE PEOPLE?

It is not enough to simply train a pool of facilitators or even to establish a facilitation program by itself. Two additional variables will be of utmost importance: the ongoing training and support of those serving as facilitators, and the "selling" of the service to the consumer. Regardless of who coordinates the program or who serves as facilitators, *somebody* is going to have to inform the public that the service is available and encourage the use of the service when it is offered. By *public* and *consumer* is meant those people who will ultimately make the decision to request or approve the participation of a neutral third party at a particular IEP meeting. In most cases, these decision makers will include the chairperson of the committee, the parents, the school administrator (principal or assistant principal), the local special education administrator, perhaps a parent advocate or attorney, and sometimes the student himself or herself.

Some personal experiences may serve to illustrate this critical juncture in the success of any facilitation program. In developing the training on which this book is based, I sought opportunities to gain "real world" experience in facilitating IEP meetings. When the logistics of time and travel permitted, I offered to facilitate at no charge provided only that the parents and chairpersons consented. At times I made this offer to whole rooms full of school professionals who were taking facilitation training, and I also notified directors of special education of my availability. Given the absence of any fees whatsoever, I expected to be flooded with requests, but this was far from the case. In fact, I received very few requests at all! However, I did receive several enthusiastic— even passionate—requests from a few chairpersons who had upcoming IEP meetings that they knew from experience were likely to be contentious. Upon advising that I would be happy to assist provided only that the parents also agreed, several unexpected developments took place that can be summarized in three categories: resistance of parents, resistance of administrators, and resistance of advisors.

In two cases, the chairpersons, very eager to have facilitation, asked their principals for permission. One was told, "No, it would be better if you just handle this yourself," and the other was told, "No, requesting a facilitator would only inflame the parent." In another case, a parent was advised by an advocate not to allow the school district to bring in "someone from the state," which, of course, I was not. In all cases, it seemed clear that fear and lack of understanding among parents, advisors, and administrators were undermining the possibility of using a service that could do no harm whatsoever and could possibly have been of great assistance to all involved. The obvious implication, then, is that for any facilitation program to be successful, a great deal of community education will be necessary, as well as securing the support of the school administration. Those making decisions will have to understand what the service is and how it can benefit them, and that they retain all the power and have nothing to lose by trying it. Without such education, the service is likely to be ignored or rejected based on nothing more than fear and limited understanding. In contrast, when support for my offer *was* well-received and did lead to facilitations was when the directors of special education saw the potential value of the service and took steps to make it possible. By personally contacting the chairpersons and parents, they took an active role themselves in helping to advertise, explain, and encourage the use of the facilitation service, and this made a decisive difference.

So, if an agency, whether local or state, wanted to launch a campaign of public information, what steps could it take? Although there might be no limit to the possibilities, several that stand out are web sites, brochures, and word-of-mouth advertising through training, announcements, and site visits.

Several state departments of education have developed web pages devoted to facilitation programs, and more are sure to emerge in the near future. A few for review include those for Wisconsin (http://www.wsems.us/training/iepfaciliation. htm), Pennsylvania (http://odr.pattan.net/earlydisputeresolution/ IEPFacilitation. aspx), and Michigan (http://www.cenmi.org/msemp/FAQ.aspx).

An information sheet about facilitated IEP meetings developed by this author and a sample agreement form are provided in Appendixes J and K. Several states have also developed brochures about the facilitation of IEP meetings, including the following:

Delaware (http://www.ipa.udel.edu/crp/IEPfacilservices.pdf)

Maryland (http://www.marylandpublicschools.org/NR/rdonlyres/
  5F4F5041-02EE-4F3A-B495-5E4B3C850D3E/13899/
  FacilitatedIEPMeetingFAQ.pdf)

Minnesota (http://education.state.mn.us/mdeprod/groups/Compliance/
  documents/FAQ/002140.pdf)

New Mexico (http://www.ped.state.nm.us/seo/dispute/FIEP%20
  HANDOUT.pdf)

North Carolina (http://www.ncpublicschools.org/docs/ec/policy/dispute/
  meeting/fiepguidelines.pdf)

North Dakota (http://www.dpi.state.nd.us/speced/resource/conflict/
  facilitation.pdf)

It is commonly accepted that word of mouth is the best form of advertising. With this in mind, those seeking to advance the use of facilitation at any level—school, district, region, or state—can begin to look at all of the available opportunities to get the message out. Aside from the obvious need for brochures and web pages, short presentations can be made at staff meetings, conferences, parent support group meetings, and in-service training events for staff. Brief audiovisual programs can be posted online, and site visits can be made to talk face to face with school and district administrators. The options are by no means limited to these. Be creative! Find what works for you.

In the sales environment, it is common practice to emphasize benefits rather than features. Thus, rather than talk about the technical details of the engine and the extensive research and development that has led to the newest model, car salesmen know the importance of talking about fuel efficiency, dollars saved each year, reduced maintenance costs, and comfort on the road. These are the things that speak to the consumers—how something will benefit them and improve their world. Facilitation can and does do this, without any question or doubt. Our job is to let the consumers know!

In closing, it should perhaps be emphasized that facilitation, with all its benefits, is still just one of many facets of a comprehensive conflict prevention and resolution program. As a consultant at many levels of special education, I am often asked to make recommendations with regard to the much broader question of how to improve school–parent relationships while at the same time minimizing and resolving conflict. Facilitation is always on that list, and yet there is much more that can and should be done. With the hope of providing ideas that may be relevant and helpful at the local level, an adapted summary of 29 points has been provided in Appendix L.

References

Abt Associates. (2002, July). *Study of state and local implementation and impact of the Individuals with Disabilities Education Act.* Retrieved January 14, 2010, from www.abt.sliidea.org/Reports/FSI_FinalRpt.doc

APR/SPP dispute resolution data summaries—Part B and Part C. (n.d.). Retrieved January 14, 2010, from http://www.directionservice.org/cadre/aprsppb.cfm

Bush, R.A.B., & Folger, J.P. (1994). *The promise of mediation: Responding to conflict through empowerment and recognition.* San Francisco: Jossey-Bass.

CADRE's national symposium on IEP facilitation. (n.d.). Retrieved January 14, 2010, from http://www.directionservice.org/cadre/conf2005

Education for All Handicapped Children Act of 1975, PL 94-142, 20 U.S.C. §§ 1400 *et seq.*

Facilitated IEP/IFSP/IIIP—Minnesota. (n.d.). Retrieved January 14, 2010, from http://www.directionservice.org/cadre/ctu/practicesA.cfm?id=59

Facilitated IEP meetings—North Carolina. (n.d.). Retrieved January 14, 2010, from http://www.directionservice.org/cadre/ctu/practicesA.cfm?id=77

Facilitated IEP project grant—Texas. (n.d.). Retrieved January 14, 2010, from http://www.directionservice.org/cadre/ctu/practicesA.cfm?id=99

Fisher, R., Ury, W., & Patton, B. (1992). *Getting to yes: Negotiating agreement without giving in* (2nd ed.). New York: Houghton Mifflin Harcourt.

IEP facilitation—North Dakota. (n.d.). Retrieved January 14, 2010, from http://www.directionservice.org/cadre/ctu/practicesA.cfm?id=89

IEP/IFSP facilitation—Michigan. (n.d.). Retrieved January 14, 2010, from http://www.directionservice.org/cadre/ctu/practicesA.cfm?id=26

Individuals with Disabilities Education Act of 1990, PL 101-476, 20 U.S.C. §§ 1400 *et seq.*

Individuals with Disabilities Education Act Amendments of 1997, PL 105-17, 20 U.S.C. §§ 1400 *et seq.*

Individuals with Disabilities Education Improvement Act of 2004, PL 108-446, 20 U.S.C. §§ 1400 *et seq.*

Martin, N.R.M. (2005). *A guide to collaboration for IEP teams.* Baltimore: Paul H. Brookes Publishing Co.

Maryland State Department of Education. (2007). *Facilitated IEP team meetings in Maryland.* Retrieved January 14, 2010, from http://www.marylandpublicschools.org/NR/rdonlyres/5F4F5041-02EE-4F3A-B495-5E4B3C850D3E/13899/FacilitatedIEPMeetingFAQ.pdf

Placement in alternative educational setting. (n.d.). Retrieved January 14, 2010, from http://idea.ed.gov/explore/view/p/%2Croot%2Cstatute%2CI%2CB%2C615%2Ck%2C

Process and practice information. (n.d.). Retrieved January 14, 2010, from http://www
.directionservice.org/cadre/ctu/processdefs.cfm?thisid=12

Rider, D., & Smith, K. (n.d.). *Lessons learned: Pennsylvania's sometimes rocky entrance into IEP
facilitation.* Retrieved January 14, 2010, from http://www.directionservice.org/cadre/
conf2005/session.cfm?seriesid=3&trackid=2

*Summary of national dispute resolution data—State numbers reported in annual performance report
(2006-07) from APR, Table 7, Section B: Mediations.* (n.d.). Retrieved January 14, 2010,
from http://www.directionservice.org/cadre/pdf/2006-2007Mediations.pdf

Wian, K. (n.d.). *Twenty questions you should answer before creating an IEP meeting facilitation
system.* Retrieved January 14, 2010, from http://www.directionservice.org/cadre/
materials/3_4/Kathy%20Wian%20Session%203.4%20-%20Handout.doc

A Exercises in Facilitation Styles

Model Responses

This exercise appears in Chapter 2, p. 23
Translate each of the following into facilitative and transformative styles:

1. None of you is following your own agreed-upon ground rules.

    Facilitative:

    a. How are you all doing with your ground rules?

    b. Is everybody feeling comfortable with the way your discussion is going?

    Transformative:

    a. Several people seem to have points they are trying to make.

    b. It seems there are several conversations going on at the same time.

2. You are really upset but keeping it all bottled up inside.

    Facilitative:

    a. You seem a little upset. Would you maybe like to talk about it?

    b. Is everyone feeling like they're getting a chance to speak and be heard?

    Transformative:

    a. Mr. Doe, you seem to have become kind of quiet.

    b. I sense some strong feelings right now.

3. You have a really bad attitude.

   Facilitative:

   a. You seem a little irritated. Would you like to maybe share your thoughts?

   b. How are you all feeling about your meeting so far?

   Transformative:

   a. This issue seems to be very important to you.

   b. Mrs. Smith, I hear you saying that this is "a total waste of time."

4. You should at least try to understand them before arguing.

   Facilitative:

   a. How are you all doing with your ground rules?

   b. What could the group do to be most helpful to you at this point?

   Transformative:

   a. Sounds like you see a better way the team could communicate, is that right?

   b. Looks like several people have thoughts they would like to have heard.

5. This is not going to be settled today.

   Facilitative:

   a. May I just ask if you feel comfortable with the progress being made today?

   b. Team, it's almost 4 P.M. Are you getting closer to an agreement?

   Transformative:

   a. Sounds like you would like the discussions to be more productive. *(pause for response)* So where would you like to go with that?

   b. I notice that some of you have put away your papers and are leaning away from the table.

B Facilitator Dos and Don'ts

1. SETTING THE STAGE

What not to do: Neglect to contact the chairperson and parent in advance; let the meeting start without an agenda, ground rules, introductions, and time projections; forget the agreement to facilitation form.

What to do: Be sure to contact the chairperson and parent; ensure introductions are made; ensure ground rules and agenda are in place; ensure time projections are made as to the probable length of the meeting and determine whether anyone may have to leave early. Also be sure to have the agreement to facilitation form read and circulated for signatures at the start of the meeting.

2. HANDLING OBJECTIONS TO THE FACILITATOR'S PRESENCE

What not to do: Justify yourself or enter into a debate; polarize the group by asking, "What do the rest of you think?"

What to do: Reflect for recognition ("Sounds like there are some questions about my being here."); probe for interests ("You must have good reasons for thinking this; would you be willing to share them?"); make a deal ("If you see me taking sides, would you be willing to point that out?"); only if pressed, ask, "Would it make sense for me to take a few moments to explain my role? Even though I work for the district . . . "

3. FACILITATOR STYLE

What not to do: Be directive; give opinions, information, or advice; reflect what you do not see; ask questions in the negative ("Don't you think . . . ?"); be transformative to a fault (be a parrot); be too involved/active and get in the way of the team.

What to do: Be transformative first; only move into the facilitative style when it becomes clear that the team members require additional support of their process (not content).

4. TORPEDOES (PERSONAL ATTACKS)

What not to do: Ignore them; delay addressing them.

What to do: Use one- or two-stage reframes (from negative to positive, from polarity to unity); reflect strong feelings for recognition; pause for reflection—how the team members feel about their meeting; ask about ground rules; "draw the fire" to yourself.

5. REFRAMES

What not to do: Underscore negativity or polarity (you versus him/her/them).

What to do: Change negatives to positives (from what they don't want to what they do want); change *you/he* to *we* (i.e., what we all want); if this is difficult, use a two-stage reframe ("So are you saying there is a different/a better/another way to be doing this? What would that look like?").

6. LOOSE ENDS

What not to do: Ignore or overlook them.

What to do: Be alert to what is left unfinished; ask such questions as "Is that issue resolved?" or "Are you all clear, then, on what you've decided about that?"

7. ADVICE, INFORMATION, AND GUIDANCE

What not to do: Give advice, guidance, or information—let others do that.

What to do: Assist the group to find its own wisdom and resources ("Sounds like there are some questions about that. How would you like to proceed? How might you best go about getting an answer? I'm only here to facilitate your process").

8. KEEPING QUIET

What not to do: Miss critical junctures for intervention; get in the way if the team members are collaborating effectively; make silence an inherent virtue (instead, know when to be active).

What to do: Listen attentively and be wise in your choices of intervention; give the team members a chance to make their own mistakes and find their own solutions, but do not let sparks lead to fires or let important issues go unnoticed or unresolved.

9. SIDE TALKING

What not to do: Ignore it.

What to do: Give the team members a chance to address it first; if they do not, decide whether this is a battle worth fighting (it may not be). If the sidetalking does seem important to address, reflect in positive terms ("I notice several conversations are going on at once" or "It seems that several people have important things to say right now").

10. INTENSE EMOTIONS (SADNESS)

What not to do: Ignore it; allow a team member to suffer.

What to do: See if the group addresses it; if not, reflect ("I notice that there are some strong feelings right now") or acknowledge ("Some of this can be very hard to hear") or offer an opportunity to share ("Would you like to maybe talk about your feelings? How can the group be most sensitive to what's going on for you?").

11. INTENSE EMOTIONS (ANGER)

What not to do: Ignore it; allow a team member to attack another; allow intensity to flare out of control.

What to do: Reflect ("I notice there are some strong feelings right now") or affirm ("You have some important points you are trying to make") or ask how the team members are feeling about their meeting or how they are doing with their ground rules; draw the fire to yourself ("Could I ask you to tell *me* your thoughts about that?").

12. IMPASSE

What not to do: Suggest or confirm failure.

What to do: Ask for help—ask the team members to articulate what it is that is making it difficult to make agreements and what they want to do as their next steps; reflect the different perspectives and ask where they want to go from here (encourage them to make agreements about their disagreements); ask if there might be any advantages or disadvantages to leaving the meeting without agreement; help clarify points of agreement and see if the team members can narrow their issues in dispute (i.e., the issues that might be left to another meeting or a higher authority); let them know that another meeting has a high probability of success, perhaps with a different facilitator.

13.   PROPOSED IEP IS NOT COMPLIANT

What not to do: Tell the team; ignore it.

What to do (in order): Reflect the agreement and wait to see if the team members themselves identify the error; ask if they all feel comfortable that their agreement is sound; propose a brief leg stretch and speak more openly in private with the chairperson; only as a last resort, remove your facilitator hat and tell them, "I feel strongly that this IEP is not compliant with the law, and I cannot remain true to an impartial facilitator's role."

14.   PROPOSED IEP IS NOT WORKABLE

What not to do: Overstep your rightful boundaries as an impartial facilitator of the team's process.

What to do: Reflect the proposals and wait to see if the team members themselves identify the possible problems; ask if they all feel comfortable that their agreement is workable; leave them free to learn by their own chosen path (or maybe they are right and it really is workable).

15.   **ENDING THE MEETING**

What not to do: Let everyone disperse without an opportunity for meaningful closure.

What to do: Ask if anyone has anything to say before the meeting is adjourned; thank everyone for their good work and for allowing you to be part of their process.

C

Sample IEP Meeting Agenda

1. Introductions

2. Purpose of the IEP meeting

3. Agenda: review and agreement

4. Probable length of meeting; will all remain for entire meeting?

5. Meeting guidelines (ground rules)

6. Statement of confidentiality

7. Review of assessment data/transition information

8. Normative testing results (national, state, or other)

9. Determination of eligibility

10. Review of previous IEP (goals and objectives)

11. Development of the IEP:

    a. Present competencies

        i. Physical

        ii. Behavioral

        iii. Academic/developmental/prevocational

    b. Develop and approve annual goals

    c. Present/proposed IEP

    d. Related services

12. Modifications/accommodations

13. Services to be provided:

    a.   Schedule of services

    b.   Appropriateness of extended school year (ESY)

        i.   Regression/recoupment cycle

        ii.   Student history

        iii. Is ESY needed?

    c.   Transportation

    d.   Assistive technology needs

14. Determination of placement

15. Assurance of least restrictive environment

16. Review and approval of minutes

17. Signatures

18. Closing questions or comments

19. Recommendations for future meetings

Note that not all steps may apply to every IEP meeting.
Please review this sample agenda with the appropriate district authorities
and modify as appropriate.

D Exercises in Reframing
Model Reframes

Imagine a participant at an IEP meeting makes the following remarks to another participant. How could the statements be reframed to make them positive ones that all members would accept? [from Chapter 3]

1. *Example:* You're being totally unreasonable and not listening to anything we say.
   Reframe: Are you saying that all perspectives should be considered?

2. *Example:* You're always so negative; you need to think more positively.
   Reframe: Is it that the child's strengths should also be recognized?

3. *Example:* You should at least want to understand before being so quick to argue.
   Reframe: Are you saying that all points should be considered before responding?

4. *Example:* You're interrupting me and raising your voice again.
   Reframe: All members having a chance to speak and be heard would be helpful, is that what you mean?

5. *Example:* Why do you always think someone's out to get you?
   Reframe: Are you saying that the members of the team should have trust in one another?

6. *Example:* Can't you just wait a minute and let me finish what I'm trying to say?
   Reframe: Is this what you mean: that everyone should have a chance to speak and be heard?

7. *Example:* I don't think she can follow all that school jargon.
   Reframe: Is it that we need to be speaking in terms that everyone can understand?

8. *Example:* Would you have the courtesy to at least not shout and call
    names?
    Reframe: Sounds like how we communicate is important, too—with
    courtesy, is that it?

9. *Example:* Maybe if you would spend more time with your child, he would
    do better.
    Reframe: Is it that the team should see a *variety* of ways in which the
    child's progress can be supported?

10. *Example:* I'm really getting tired of your threatening to get a lawyer.
    Reframe: It could be helpful to have commitment to collaboration and
    trusting that the team can work things out, am I understanding your
    thought?

Facilitation Intervention Options

TRANSFORMATIVE

1. *Repeat for recognition:* Repeat exactly what you hear the speaker saying. Example: "Your child 'is going to remain in the general classroom no matter what.' Is that right?"

2. *Reframe for recognition:* Clarify a feeling, perception, intention, or interest in positive terms that all can endorse. Example: "Whatever it takes, the student should have the most appropriate placement, right?"

3. *Reflect for recognition:* Reflect the process that you observe, either to the group ("There seem to be a lot of strong feelings at the moment") or to the individual ("Mrs. Smith, you seem perhaps a little uncomfortable").

4. *Empower:* Ask questions that provide an opportunity to choose, either to the group ("Where do you all want to go with that?") or to the individual ("Where do you want to go with that?").

FACILITATIVE

5. *Pause for reflection:* Give the group members a chance to consider their process. Example: "May I just touch base and ask how you all are feeling about your meeting so far?" or "Is everyone feeling like they've had a chance to speak and be heard?"

6. *Ask about ground rules:* Invite reflection about agreements made earlier. Example: "How are you all doing with your ground rules?"

7. *Hold a focus:* Ask for more two times to assist in clarifying perspectives and airing feelings. Example: "Would you like to say some more about that?" (allow response); then, "Is there anything else you'd like to share about this?" (allow response).

8. *Probe for underlying interests:* Explore reasons so as to gain understanding. Example: "You must have good reasons for that. Can you help the group understand your thoughts?" or "What do you see happening if you all go that route?"

9. *Acknowledge:* Recognize a possible situation, feeling, or thought. Example: "Mrs. Jones, some of those suggestions must be really hard to hear" or "So much information can sometimes be kind of overwhelming."

10. *Affirm:* Use praise as a means of support. Example: "I can see that you are very committed to your child's education" or "You must have good reasons for feeling that way."

11. *Refocus:* Gently lead a participant back to the issue at hand. Example: "Could I ask you to summarize the key points you'd like the group to understand about this?"

12. *When in doubt, check it out:* If a possible situation warrants confirmation, ask. Example: "Mr. Worczyk, are you maybe a little upset right now?" or "How are you feeling about that suggestion?"

13. *Ask for help:* Ask the individual or the team for options or suggestions. Example: "What could the group do to be most helpful to you right now?" or (to the team) "What might help you all move forward at this point?"

14. *Apologize:* Recognize a possible wrongdoing, even when it may not be your fault. Example: "I am really sorry if I've been taking their side. I apologize for whatever I may have done to give that impression."

15. *Make a deal:* Ask the other party or parties to agree to speak up if they perceive a certain behavior or have a negative feeling. Example: "Mr. Green, if you see me taking sides, would you be willing to point it out and let me know?"

16. *Play with the time shape:* Propose a short-term solution to be reevaluated later. Example: "What would you think about trying this idea for, say, a month or so, and then, if it isn't going well, maybe change it at your next meeting?"

17. *Share your good intention:* Explain why you are saying what you are. Example: "I really want you to feel safe to express your thoughts and feelings, Mrs. Nakamura."

18. *Point at self:* Let any perceived ignorance or impatience be directed at you to avoid putting anyone else in an uncomfortable position. Example: "I'm not sure I am following you, Mr. Kumar."

19. *Redirect (draw the fire):* Ask that the conversation be directed to you as a means of reducing the intensity toward a member of the team. Example: "Mr. Benik, may I interrupt you? Could I ask you to tell me more about that?"

Directive—*Do Not Enter!*

- *Instruct/explain:* "Well, under district policy..."

- *Give advice or expert opinion:* "In my opinion, you should..."

- *Tell:* "Team, you need to remember your ground rule about..."

- *Wolves in sheep's clothing (veiled attempts at giving information):* "Do you think reviewing your ground rules would be a good idea about now?" or "I can't tell you what to do, but doesn't the law have some language about that?" or "Wouldn't it make sense to get some more testing?"

General Rule:
How can I make that statement more transformative?

F

Exercises in Identifying Intervention Options

Model Responses

For each of the following examples, identify the interventions being used and then critique the style to improve it, if necessary. [from Chapter 5]

1. "I'm feeling a little lost. [pointing at self] When you say 'he only cares about the money,' is it that you're not trusting the real motivation? [reframing for recognition] Can you help me understand what you mean here?" [pointing at self and asking for help]

The first pointing at self does not appear to be supporting the collaboration of the team. It therefore may be unnecessary and might even appear critical of how the team has been communicating. The reframe is still very much in polarity (you against him) and is also underscoring a negative, neither of which is recommended. The asking for help is fine, but the words "help me" represents, again, pointing at self in a way that seems to aggrandize the facilitator; saying, "Can you help the team?" or "Can you help the group?" would be preferred. A recommended way to express these same good intentions might look like this:

"Are you saying that decisions should be based on what's best for the child more than anything else? [reframing, positively and in unity] Can you help the team understand your thoughts here?" [asking for help]

2. "There seem to be some strong feelings right now. [reflecting for recognition] I hear a lot of interruptions and a few choice words. [reflecting for recognition] Anyone else seeing that?" [checking it out]

The first reflection seems appropriate. The second, in contrast, evaluates the words being used and seems to criticize the group members for their interruptions and "choice words." Such evaluation is directive in style. Asking if anyone else is seeing the same things is probably not necessary and, because it follows an implied criticism, might seem to be a way of asking the group members to fess up to their misdeeds or to ally themselves with the facilitator against those who are "misbehaving." An alternative might be the following, although it might not be necessary to string all three reflections together—one or two might be enough:

"There seem to be a lot of strong feelings right now. I notice several conversations going on at the same time, and several people seem to have important points they are trying to make."

3.   "Say some more about that. [probing for interests or asking for help] This seems to be a very important issue for you [reflecting for recognition], and I want to be sure I understand where you're coming from." [pointing at self and sharing a good intention]

The phrase "Say some more about that" is very directive, clearly telling the speaker what to do next. The reflection is fine. The good intention might be more appropriate if spoken for the team's, rather than the facilitator's, understanding. After all, the facilitator's only role is to support the team members to do *their* work. An alternative might be the following:

"This seems to be a very important issue for you." [pause to see what the speaker or team does next; if nothing productive happens, then continue with] "Can you help the team understand your thoughts?"

4.   "Mr. Harris, I'm not really comfortable with the way that was said. [pointing at self] I know you have an important point you are trying to make. [reflecting for recognition and affirming "important"] Could you say it again, please, without the swear words?" [asking for help]

This is a good example of an inappropriate use of self. Whether the facilitator is comfortable or not is of no relevance whatsoever because it has nothing to do with the group's collaborative process. Moreover, the intervention is obviously evaluative; it implies that the speaker has said something wrong. The reflection and affirmation are fine, but the asking for help is also directive. Here is an alternative, and after he responds, the next step would probably be a one- or two-stage reframe to capture and make more positive the torpedoes that Mr. Harris has been launching with his swearing:

"Mr. Harris, I can see you have an important point you are trying to make. Could you help the team understand your thoughts?"

5.   "This seems to be really hard for you [reflecting for recognition], so what would you like to do next? [empowering] Would you like to maybe take a break? Could a break maybe be helpful at this point?" [asking for help]

Reflecting for recognition is almost always a safe and appropriate choice, and the example here might be just fine had the facilitator stopped right there. A very common tendency of new facilitators is to quickly link the reflection with the empowerment, as illustrated in this example. It would have been much better to leave a reasonable pause before adding the empowering question of "So what would you like to do next?" The asking for help may look just fine on the surface, and yet it is really covertly directive because it so clearly suggests a right answer (to take a break). One of the ways to guard against this "leading the witness" is to offer *several* options; for example, "Would you like to take a break or perhaps talk about your feelings, or maybe just have the group continue on? What would be most helpful to you right now?" Such a series of possibilities would be very appropriate coming from any member of *the team,* but not necessarily from the facilitator. The facilitator would be on safer turf to simply ask the individual, "What would be most helpful to you right now?" or ask the team if any members might have a suggestion as to what might be helpful at this time. This scenario phrased more in keeping with the transformative and facilitative styles might look like this:

"This seems to be really hard for you." [reflecting for recognition, then a long pause to see how the speaker responds; if the speaker remains silent and obviously troubled, the next step might be] "I'd really like to be helpful in some way." [sharing a good intention] "What could the team do to be most sensitive to your feelings at this point?" [asking for help]

6.   "Team, I'm sorry to interrupt you. [apologizing] Just wanted to check in and see how we are feeling about our discussions so far. [pausing for reflection] I know I've been feeling a little uncomfortable with the tensions [pointing at self], and some of the ground rules are not being followed." [reflecting for recognition]

The opening apology may be fine. Pausing for reflection is also a fine and generally appropriate intervention. The use of the words *we* and *our* is not inherently wrong or counter to recommended methods, although it is certainly more facilitative in style than transformative. Using *we* and *our* obviously includes the facilitator in the group being referred to, and this is something the facilitator should only do with care and purpose. In general, *you* and *the team* may be more appropriate, because the facilitator's presence is only meant to support the members. This confusion of purpose becomes more evident when the facilitator adds, "I've been feeling a little uncomfortable with the tensions." Not only does this seem evaluative, as if the team has been doing something wrong, but the facilitator's feelings are really irrelevant; the more important issue is how the team members are feeling. The final reflecting for recognition is clearly evaluative—criticizing the group for not following their ground rules. In addition, a cardinal rule has been broken by the facilitator when the reflecting occurs in the negative, what the mirror does *not* see (that the rules are not being followed). A better way to address these same issues might be as follows:

"Team, I'm sorry to interrupt you." [apologizing] "Just wanted to check in and see how you all are feeling about your discussions so far." [pausing for reflection]

The facilitator would probably do just fine to stop there, but if for any reason these interventions were not enough to restore collaboration, the following would be more in keeping with the models presented in this book: "There seem to be some tensions in the room." [reflecting for recognition] "May I just touch base and ask how you all are doing with your ground rules?" [asking about ground rules]

G Exercises in Process Intervention

Model Responses

For each scenario, imagine that you are the facilitator and consider 1) how you would intervene, 2) why you would choose that option, and 3) what you would do if your chosen intervention does not seem to be enough to restore collaboration or otherwise address the challenge. [from Chapter 5]

1.   When discussing proposed ground rules, one participant says, "I'm not agreeing to turn off my cell phone."

There is rarely a single right answer to any question of what a skilled facilitator would or should do. Instead, there are always a number of options; the choice will depend on the facilitator's professional judgment—not in the sense of judging (evaluating) but in the sense of wisdom and expertise. In this example, the facilitator should certainly not debate the question or ask how the others feel, which would polarize the group into those for and those against. A recommended practice might be to first stay transformative with a simple reflection for recognition: "It's important that your cell phone be on during this meeting, right?" Hopefully this will lead the speaker to clarify why this is so, perhaps because she has a sick child at home and is waiting for a call from the doctor's office. Such an explanation might lead others to agree under the circumstances or to ask that she consider putting her phone on silent mode. If this intervention does not seem to be helpful, a next step might be to probe for interests: "You must have good reasons for wanting to keep your cell phone on, am I right?" Yet another possibility would be to simply hold up for recognition the different views being expressed and then to empower the group: "So it's important to keep it on in case there is a call from the doctor. And it might best support the meeting if the phones were off. So where do you all want to go with that?"

2.   In the course of conversation, you notice that voices are rising, interruptions are becoming more frequent, and the meeting is becoming a shouting match.

Facilitators can always start transformatively with a simple process reflection, such as "There seem to be a lot of strong feelings in the room right now." This will probably lead the members to recognize their behavior and begin to talk about their feelings rather than act them out through continued shouting and interruptions. Perhaps they will say something such as "Well, yes I do have strong feelings. My child has a right to a least restrictive environment…" If this first intervention is not enough to restore collaboration, a pause for reflection might be helpful ("How are you all feeling about your meeting so far?"), or ask about the ground rules ("May I just ask how are you all doing with your ground rules?").

3.   You see that a lot of acronyms and jargon are being used and have reason to think that one or more of the participants are lost.

This would be a great place to point at self rather than imply that anyone is wrong for using jargon or that anyone else is unaware of what the jargon means. Thus, "I am not sure I am following you. Could I ask you to clarify for me what you meant by 'OHI' and 'cognitive deficits'?" The only purpose for using these "I" terms is to support the *team's* collaboration without implying criticism. If this should fail to address the issue, as evidenced by continuing use of jargon and continued puzzled looks, the facilitator could suggest a pause for reflection: "May I just ask how you all feel your meeting is going at this point?" Another option is "when in doubt, check it out": "May I just check in with everyone and see if you all are comfortable with the discussion and clear on the terminology?"

4.   You notice that one participant is dominating the conversation and that all others tend to direct their comments and questions to her.

Rather than confront the one who is speaking or the ones who are not, and thereby imply that they should be doing something different, a pause for reflection might be helpful: "May I just ask how you all are feeling about your meeting so far?" Perhaps one or more members will comment on how quiet so many of the members seem to be. Another option if this does not seem helpful is to check it out by asking, "Just wanted to check in and ask if everyone is feeling comfortable that they are having a chance to share any concerns or questions they may have."

5.   You notice that the parents tend to be very quiet; you sense that they are not happy but are just not speaking up and sharing what they think and feel.

A pause for reflection might give the parents an easy opening to share what they are feeling or thinking without confronting them with their silence. Thus, asking the group, "How are you all feeling about your meeting so far?" might be enough to draw the parents into the conversation. If that fails, check it out by asking, "Mr. and Mrs. Smith, I was just wondering if you are feeling okay about the way the meeting is going at this point?"

6.   The committee's chairperson has a very authoritative style, and others seem to be afraid to speak up and share.

This is a very similar scenario to Example 4, and the interventions could be exactly the same. Rather than imply criticism of the one who seems authoritative or the ones who are more reserved, a pause for reflection might be all that is needed: "May I just ask how you all are feeling about your meeting so far?" Perhaps one or more members will comment on how few of the members are willing to say anything. Another option if this does not seem helpful is to check it out: "Just wanted to touch base and ask if everyone is feeling comfortable that they are having a chance to share if they want to." At every moment, this is *their* meeting and these are *their* choices to be made, so the facilitator must not get too attached to what the members decide to do.

7.   The mother becomes tearful and others seem uncomfortable; the chairperson keeps the discussions going as if nothing were wrong.

Here the facilitator might lead with a simple reflection for recognition: "I notice some strong feelings in the room right now." A reason to choose this option is that it is very mild and gives the team members full freedom to recognize their circumstances and perhaps choose a different way of responding to the mother. If the team continues to ignore her, perhaps because of discomfort with strong emotion or simply because they do not know *how* to respond, the mother should not be left to suffer on her own and without support. If the team does not respond to her, the facilitator could simply share a good intention and ask for help: "Mrs. Jones, I want to be sensitive to your feelings right now. How could the team be most helpful to you at this time?"

8.   A lot of time is spent repeating the same point at issue and the same demands and arguments; no progress is being made.

A pause for reflection might assist the team to stand back and take a look at its process rather than remain so focused on the repeated demands: "Could I just ask you how you all feel your meeting is going at this point?" When, as is likely, the members say that they are not getting anywhere, the facilitator could then ask for help: "Any ideas what might help you move forward?" When members suggest open minds, or a greater willingness to listen, or additional data, or whatever it may be, the facilitator can highlight these suggestions and help the group to consider making new agreements: "So it sounds like some of you think that open minds would be helpful. Others seem to think additional data are necessary. Where would you like to go with that?" (repeating for recognition, then empowering).

9.   It seems clear that this meeting is not going to result in agreement.

When it seems clear that the meeting *may* not end in agreement, the facilitator can simply reflect the facts (but not a prediction) for recognition and check it out: "Team, I notice it's almost 5 p.m. Are you feeling like you are getting close to settling the issues?" When the participants say no, the facilitator could ask for help ("Any ideas about what seems to be making it difficult?") and thus encourage the team members to verbalize their perspectives (we're tired, it's late, we don't have the data, we have different interpretations of the data, we have closed minds, etc.). The facilitator could then hold up (repeat) their comments for recognition and then either ask where the team wants to go from there (empowerment) or ask for suggestions as to what the team members think would be helpful (asking for help).

10.   You suspect that the proposed individualized education program (IEP) is not compliant with federal law or district policy.

The first step at such a time might be to just repeat the agreement the team members are making and see if they themselves notice the violation: "Team, it sounds like your agreement would be to have the child spend an hour in the storage room, unsupervised, if the teacher finds his behavior unmanageable, is that right?" (repeating for recognition). If no one indicates any concerns, the facilitator can check it out by asking, "Are you all comfortable that this is a good plan and a workable arrangement?" If that fails, the facilitator could propose a brief break and talk more directly with the chairperson in private. If, as seems very unlikely, the team continues to agree on a plan that is obviously in violation of the law, and all of these steps have been taken to no avail, then the facilitator might have to acknowledge his or her bias at this point and recuse himself or herself, perhaps by saying, "Team, I have to acknowledge to you that I really cannot in good faith support a proposal that I know is in violation of the law. I therefore believe that at this point I must withdraw from being your facilitator." Again, this is presented as a theoretical more than a likely event.

This scenario raises some interesting ethical dilemmas. Can the facilitator really be party to a decision that he or she *knows* is in violation of the law without carrying ethical responsibility on a personal level and perhaps legal responsibility if he or she is employed by a school district? If the facilitator were subpoenaed into court (in a due process hearing) to answer to a known violation of federal law, would the hearing officer accept "I was only there as a facilitator"? This has probably not yet been put to the legal test. It is recommended that the facilitator seek the advice of his or her district authorities with regard to the limits of legal and ethical responsibility if such a situation were to arise.

As a final note in this regard, some states are making it a standard procedure that all parties sign a statement of agreement at the start of the meeting. Part of the agreement's language has to do with limiting the responsibilities of the facilitator. A sample form is presented in Appendix K.

11.   An agreement has been reached, but you have reason to believe that the plan is not workable and that the participants are just agreeing so they can be done and leave.

This scenario is very similar to the previous example, except no violation of law is suspected. The intervention might once again begin with simply repeating for recognition: "Sounds like you are in agreement that the teacher will send detailed daily reports to the parents as to classroom attendance, participation, and behavior, and the parents will ensure completion of all homework assignments, supported by an hour a day of in-home tutoring, is that right?" If all parties agree, then the facilitator can check it out by saying, "Does everyone feel comfortable that this is a workable plan?" If the parties continue to agree, then the facilitator should accept their decision—it is not the facilitator's place to evaluate it. It may be that if the plan is *not* workable, the team members will benefit greatly from what they learn in trying it out. It may also be that the plan is actually more workable than the facilitator believes.

12.   When you ask if any members have anything they might like to say before closing, you sense that some participants are upset but won't say anything.

The facilitator might begin with a simple reflection for recognition: "I sense some discomfort in the room right now." If no one speaks up, the facilitator can check it out by asking, "Is everyone comfortable if you end your meeting at this time?" Or he or she can reflect for recognition by saying, "Seems like everyone has said all they wish to say for today, am I right?" If the team members still remain silent, the facilitator can accept it; recognition and empowerment have been offered, and the decision is entirely theirs to make.

Note that many of the issues addressed in this exercise are included in the summary of facilitator dos and don'ts in Appendix B.

H | Dealing with Impasse
A Summary of Options

From Chapter 6:

Momentary Impasse (agreement may still be possible)

1. Reflect and acknowledge ("You all seem to be having a tough time right now.")

2. Ask for help; invite suggestions as to the source of the impasse (e.g., lack of information, different interpretations of behavior, hot tempers, surprising information, hurt feelings, mistrust, different understandings of law and policies)

3. Retrace the day's progress; review what has been agreed and what remains undecided

4. Play with the time shape of a proposal ("What if you were to try it for, say, a month, and if it wasn't working, you could reassess and perhaps modify the plan? Does that idea have any value? What do you all think?")

5. Build in guarantees and contingencies ("If that happens, then…")

6. Probe for the benefits of reaching agreement today (shared interests) and the costs of leaving without agreement (shared risks)

Fatal Impasse (it is clear that agreement will not be reached)

7. Propose another meeting, perhaps with a different facilitator

8. Propose mediation

9. Narrow the issues in dispute by summarizing the agreements made (perhaps in writing) and highlighting the points left undecided

10. Invite agreements about the disagreements—how do the team members wish to proceed?

Twenty Questions You Should Answer

Before Creating an IEP Meeting Facilitation System

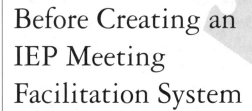

Reprinted with the kind permission of Kathy Wian of the University of Delaware Conflict Resolution Program. [see Chapter 7]

1. What is the purpose for creating an IEP meeting facilitation system and expected outcomes/definitions of success?

2. Who will manage/oversee the IEP meeting facilitation system?

3. How will the system be funded?

4. What are the role and responsibilities of the IEP meeting facilitator?

5. How will the system/program be marketed to schools, districts, parents, advocates, mentors, other interested parties?

6. How will the system be evaluated and what information will be tracked?

   a. Number of cases?

   b. Number of meetings?

   c. Hours spent per meeting or per case?

   d. Issues discussed?

   e. School, district, or county using the service?

   f. Outcome of each meeting?

   g. Whether the team reached consensus on the IEP?

   h. Satisfaction level of all meeting participants?

   i. Facilitator's performance?

    j.   Other indicators for success?

    k.   Follow-up after the case?

    l.   Is this system tracked in conjunction with other resolution systems?

7.   Who can request an IEP meeting facilitator?

8.   How does someone request an IEP meeting facilitator?

9.   What is the internal process once a request is received?

    a.   What forms will be used?

    b.   Who will conduct the "intake" and what information will be gathered?

    c.   What is the minimum amount of time needed to meet the request?

    d.   What information will be maintained in the case file and for how long?

10.   Do all parties have to agree to use an IEP meeting facilitator?

    a.   Will there be a pre-meeting agreement form that is signed by the parent and school/district representative agreeing to use a facilitator?

11.   How will the confidentiality of the student and family be maintained at the time of request?

    a.   What information may be shared by the school if it is the requesting party?

    b.   What information may be shared with the facilitator prior to the meeting?

12.   Is the commitment of a facilitator unlimited once he or she facilitates a meeting?

    a.   Under what circumstances may the facilitator schedule him- or herself for another meeting?

    b.   When should they not commit to another meeting?

    c.   Will there be a cap placed on the number of meetings a facilitator may attend for each case?

13.   Must there be a dispute in order for a facilitator to attend an IEP meeting?

    a.   If so, how do you define "dispute"?

    b.   Do all parties have to agree that there is a dispute?

14.   When can a request for an IEP meeting facilitator be denied?

15. Who decides which facilitator gets which case?

16. Who will be trained to be an IEP meeting facilitator?

    a. What criteria will be used in selecting potential facilitators?

    b. What qualifications are required to be a facilitator?

    c. How many facilitators are needed?

17. Once someone is trained as a facilitator, what criteria will be used to decide if he or she has the skills to facilitate an IEP meeting?

18. What do the IEP meeting facilitators need to know about confidentiality?

19. How will facilitators be evaluated and how often?

20. How will facilitators be kept abreast of changes that occur in special education, particularly the law?

    a. Will ongoing training be offered?

    b. Will it be mandatory?

Comments and suggestions are welcome and may be directed to:
Kathy Wian
University of Delaware
Conflict Resolution Program
177 Graham Hall, Academy Street
Newark, DE 19716
302-831-2927
kwian@udel.edu
http://www.directionservice.org/cadre/materials/3_4/Kathy%20Wian%20
Session%203.4%20-%20Handout.doc; reprinted by permission.

J

Sample Information Sheet for a Facilitated IEP Meeting

What Is a "Facilitated IEP Meeting"?

Facilitation is a process in which a trained and impartial person who is not a member of the committee assists the IEP team to communicate effectively and work toward agreements with which the members can all feel comfortable. The facilitator is not a decision maker or an advisor, and he or she does not endorse or sign the IEP.

What Are the Benefits of Facilitation?

Facilitation takes place during regularly scheduled IEP meetings and helps ensure a safe and respectful environment in which all members can feel welcome to share their perspectives. Among the many benefits that can be expected are

- A positive climate for discussion
- More focused and efficient use of time

- Greater clarity and mutual understanding

- Improved team spirit and working relationships

- Increased "ownership" of the agreements made

- Reduced risk of bad feelings, tensions, and conflict

- An increased probability of reaching an agreed-upon IEP

- Better serving the student for whom the team is meeting

When Is Facilitation Recommended?

Facilitation can be used whenever an IEP team wants to improve team spirit and effectiveness. When conflicts have developed, facilitation can help defuse tensions, improve communications, and restore trust and more positive working relationships. It can also be used when no conflict exists at all, to ensure better use of time, more effective communication, and more productive meetings.

What Happens Once Facilitation Is Requested?

Once facilitation is requested, an assigned facilitator will contact the chairperson and the parents by telephone to confirm the agreement to facilitation, verify the meeting time and place, and answer any questions they may have. An agreement form for facilitation is signed by all participants at the start of the IEP meeting.

Are There Any Costs or Downsides to Facilitation?

The costs of facilitation, if any, are paid by the school district. There are no known downsides because no options are lost by agreeing to facilitation; the participants have nothing to lose and a great deal to gain.

Who Are the Facilitators?

In most cases, the facilitators are school district professionals who are already very familiar with the IEP process. In addition, they have received specialized training in how to be impartial and how to support productive dialogue among IEP team members. Although they may be employed by a school district, their role at the meeting is to support the process of the team, not to give advice or make decisions. They are committed to a neutral role, and any participants are welcome to speak up if at any time they perceive the facilitator as stepping out of an impartial role.

Whom Can I Call for More Information?

For more information or to schedule a facilitation, contact:

K | Sample Agreement Form for a Facilitated IEP Meeting

Location _____ Date _____

By signing below, the participants at this facilitated individualized education program (IEP) meeting understand and agree that

1. The purpose of facilitation is to assist the committee to work together effectively for the benefit of the student

2. The facilitator will not give advice, does not sign or approve the IEP, and will not express opinions about what is right or wrong. Rather, the facilitator will help the members of the committee make their own decisions by supporting their communication

3. The participants will not ask that the facilitator or any observer (if applicable) testify or be subpoenaed to testify about what was said during the facilitated meeting

4. The facilitator and any observers agree to confidentiality and will not voluntarily testify or report on anything said during this facilitated meeting UNLESS one of the participants makes a threat of physical harm or reveals information of child abuse or elder abuse

5. The school district remains responsible for the provision of the special education and related services developed through this facilitated IEP process

1. _____   _____
   Printed name and role   Signature

2. _____   _____
   Printed name and role   Signature

3. _____   _____
   Printed name and role   Signature

4. _____   _____
   Printed name and role   Signature

continue on reverse if necessary

L A Broad-Based Proposal for Conflict Reduction

This appendix is adapted from summaries I have provided to school districts encountering particularly high levels of conflict and litigation in special education. It is a work in progress, by no means finalized or complete. It is included here only for the purpose of stimulating thought and discussion in the hope of being helpful at the local level.

Parent Training

1. **Create a brochure for parents about what to do if they are unhappy.** Perhaps include testimonials from those parents who have used collaborative problem-solving approaches with positive results.

2. **Train parents** in collaboration and conflict prevention. Offer programs at their usual meeting places, such as support group meetings and parent forums. Offer training in Spanish or other languages, as appropriate.

3. **Develop and promote parent training videos** that can be posted on the Internet and/or distributed as CDs or DVDs. Appeal to parents to consider non-adversarial options that help reduce costs while preserving positive school–parent relationships. Provide relevant local and statewide statistics. Discuss the benefits of cooperative problem solving, perhaps with representatives from family resource centers or local advocacy groups, as parents often do not realize the broader implications of due process hearings and formal complaints or their non-adversarial alternatives. As examples, see the Flash videos on listening and understanding interests by the Center for Appropriate Dispute Resolution in Special Education

at http://www.directionservice.org/cadre. Other parent training videos are posted in both English and Spanish at www.4accord.com/videos.html.

Parent Advocacy

4. **Provide district-sponsored training** of parent advocates in the vision of partnership that is the intent of special education law. Discuss how to work collaboratively using principled negotiation, diplomacy, facilitation, mediation, and so forth.

5. **Maintain a recommended list** of those advocates who have completed the district's training, endorsed a published code of ethics, and supplied letters of reference. Allow for grievance to the district or some professional body if advocates are found to be adversarial or unprofessional. Advertise the list to parents, and give advocates a reason to want to be on it (although parents can still choose any advocate they wish).

6. **Develop an informative brochure for parents** regarding how to choose an advocate. See http://www.fcsn.org/pti/advocacy/advocacy_brochure.pdf for an example developed by the Federation for Children with Special Needs and the Massachusetts Department of Education.

7. **Certify advocates**. Encourage professional organizations to lobby the state legislature to pass legislation requiring professional advocates to 1) complete, for example, 40 hours of training in the collaborative vision of the Individuals with Disabilities Education Improvement Act; 2) represent a published code of ethics; and 3) hold themselves accountable to some professional body. Allow schools to bar admission to individualized education program (IEP) meetings for those professional advocates who are not on the state list.

Collaborative Means of Dispute Resolution

8. **Provide ombudsmen,** perhaps using trained parent liaisons, case managers, or other existing school personnel. Show parents that they have somewhere to go where district staff will listen and assist when they have concerns.

9. **Encourage expanded use of state-provided mediation,** especially when it can be used without lawyers becoming involved. Train district

personnel in how to use the mediation process for healing, building trust, and strengthening communications for the future (i.e., how to use it for growth and true resolution and not just settlement).

10.   **Use facilitators at resolution meetings** by agreement of the parent and chairperson.

11.   **Develop local mediation** on a less formal level (not just state-provided mediation), perhaps using local dispute resolution center mediators or IEP facilitators (it would be easy to train them to do mediation if they understand facilitation).

12.   **Develop and promote short Internet infomercials** on mediation, facilitation, and other alternative dispute resolution options available in the district. Each video could perhaps be only 5 minutes in length.

13.   **Encourage school professionals and parents to use facilitation, ombudsmen, and mediators** through site visits, brochures, training segments, conference announcements, and so forth.

14.   **Make site visits to school and district administrators** to promote the use of facilitation and collaborative means of dispute resolution.

15.   **Create a district "special review board"** to serve as an informal and local complaint investigation or "due process hearing." Give the board the authority to intervene if schools are deemed in violation (not in any way replacing state-provided recourses).

16.   **Provide a "scholarship" option.** Allow parents to opt out of public school placement and receive an appropriate sum to fund the private education of their choice.

Intercooperation and Mutual Support

17.   **Create parent–school teams for training.** Give parents a voice and a role to play in this process.

18.   **Coordinate a unified task force** with parent resources. Make parents partners. Network with those to whom parents look for guidance. Assign staff and parent representatives to specific focus groups pertaining to areas of identified need. Encourage local advocacy and parent support groups to participate.

19. **Create opportunities for positive interaction with parents.** Make them your allies (rebuild trust, provide child care, help with transportation, show a willingness to be responsive).

20. **Sponsor forums for school–parent dialogue,** perhaps monthly. Provide these opportunities in Spanish and other languages, or with interpretation, as well.

Litigious Law Firms

21. **Seek the advice of counsel** and explore options with the state bar, if necessary. File a grievance with the bar against attorneys who are deemed unethical, bring frivolous cases, or needlessly expand legitimate cases.

22. **Request a meeting with administrative law judges.** Ask what they would recommend for attorneys who are in clear violation of the spirit and intention of the law.

23. **Use the media**—newspaper articles, radio or TV interviews, letters to the editor, or paid advertisements—to raise awareness of the damage to the community of excessive parent–school conflict.

24. **Set a precedent** by holding parents and their attorneys to the letter of the law, which says that they can be responsible for the district's cost of defense in a frivolous action:

> . . .the court, in its discretion, may award reasonable attorneys' fees as part of the costs to:…A prevailing SEA or LEA [state or local education agency] against the attorney of a parent, or against the parent, if the parent's request for a due process hearing or subsequent cause of action was presented for any improper purpose, such as to harass, to cause unnecessary delay, or to needlessly increase the cost of litigation. (20 U.S.C. 1415[i][3][B][i])

25. **Refuse to settle** out of court. Parents generally have a very small chance of actually going to a hearing after requesting one. Beware the false economy of teaching parents that if they do not get what they want at IEP meetings, they can simply file for due process and get it from a district's unwritten policy of out-of-court settlement. (The percentage of filed due process requests that actually result in a hearing varies enormously from state to state: California, approximately 3%–5%; Texas, approximately 12%; Washington, DC, approximately 78%. These statistics can be determined by comparing the number of hearings requested and the

number adjudicated according to a state's Annual Performance Report, which can be found online at http://www.directionservice.org/cadre/aprsppb.cfm.)

Preventative Staff Development Training

26. **Provide wide-scale training** of school personnel in collaboration, diplomacy, effective communication, and conflict resolution. Ensure that general classroom teachers become involved as well—not just special education and administrative staff.

27. **Make collaboration and conflict prevention training mandatory for all principals.**

28. **Include collaboration and conflict prevention training for newly hired principals** and superintendents through "principals' academies," if such training programs are a prerequisite for the position. If they are not a prerequisite, make them one.

29. **Train staff using online programs** so they can attend at their own convenience. Consider that all those who attend IEP meetings are expected to work collaboratively toward consensus with a minimum of conflict, and yet the vast majority nationwide have never been taught how to do this.

Index

Boxes, figures, and tables are indicated by *b, f,* and *t,* respectively.